SOUTH AFRICA:
Nation or Nations?

by DAVID L. NIDDRIE

Professor of Geography
University of Florida

A SEARCHLIGHT ORIGINAL

under the general editorship of

G. ETZEL PEARCY
The [illegible]rapher
U. S. Department of State

GEORGE W. HOFFMAN
Professor of Geography
University of Texas

D. VAN NOSTRAND COMPANY, INC.

PRINCETON, NEW JERSEY

TORONTO MELBOURNE LONDON

Van Nostrand Regional Offices:
New York, Chicago, San Francisco

D. Van Nostrand Company, Ltd., *London*

D. Van Nostrand Company (Canada), Ltd., *Toronto*

D. Van Nostrand Australia Pty. Ltd., *Melbourne*

Published simultaneously in Canada by
D. Van Nostrand Company (Canada), Ltd.

Library of Congress Catalog Card No. 68-29878

PRINTED IN THE UNITED STATES OF AMERICA

Preface

South Africa has occupied a painfully prominent place on the international scene ever since 1946, when the delegation from India at the United Nations made a bitter attack on that country's attitudes towards its East Indian residents. The gradual accretion of independent African and Asian nations to the General Assembly has resulted in widening debate, active conflict in certain international bodies, and increasing impatience with a white minority which refuses point-blank to modify its policies of racial segregation.

As these attacks mount, it becomes more and more difficult to differentiate fact from fiction or logic from emotional tirade. The United Nations General Assembly in 1967 considered economic sanctions and possibly even military invasion as coercive methods of effecting change in the coming years, and in 1968 is concentrating on ways and means of bringing the South-West African Mandated Territory under the control of the U.N. Trusteeship Council. It therefore becomes vital for all concerned to comprehend fully what is involved in these successive steps. With the closing of the Suez Canal in June of 1967, all maritime nations also became embarrassingly aware of the essential role of South African ports in victualing and re-fueling their ships on the Cape route. For embargoers and boycotters it is an agonizing choice.

In 1961 a frustrated news editor of a national newspaper in the United States instructed his staff to ignore South Africa in the future because it had obviously become "just another banana republic" and was no longer worth any space in the paper. Events have proved him wrong, mainly because he had oversimplified his views, selecting facts which fitted perhaps the tarnished image of Latin

American political gyrations, and because he had tried to draw direct analogies with the racial situation in the United States.

South Africa has remained obdurately stable despite Afro-Asian diplomatic and economic pressures and massive campaigns on the part of Russian and Chinese communist-trained saboteurs, who use liberal and dissident fronts within the country to create industrial and political chaos. The country has the confidence of international investors and bankers; it is fiscally incorruptible and has paid off all its active lend-lease and other war debts. It receives no technical aid or financial support from the United States or from any other country.

Annual predictions of proletarian or peasant revolution, mostly based on faulty intelligence and interpretation, have failed to materialize so far. Accused of being a police state, South Africa nonetheless permits a wide range of dissent in a free press. Considered by international labor organizations to be oppressive in its attitudes towards labor, free movement of peoples, and the franchise, it has an outstanding system of factory, industrial, and prisoner reform legislation, as well as effective wage negotiation machinery largely divorced from classical trade unionism. It attracts large numbers of foreign Africans to its economic honeypot. It is also busy granting internal self-government to several of its tribal "nations," and is spending vast sums on rehabilitating Bantu lands and people.

There is, in fact, an anomaly or contradiction buried in every assertion made about South Africa. In an attempt to explain a few of these, the author has tried to interpret the environmental, human, and economic resources of the country both in space and time. Political personalities have been practically excluded from the scene, despite the important part which many of them have played in the country's development. (A Selected Bibliography goes some way toward filling this gap for those who wish to know more about Cecil Rhodes, Paul Kruger, Louis Botha, and Jan Smuts.) Moral strictures have likewise been avoided in view of the fact that vast armies of authors and pamphleteers have already found this a highly profitable field to exploit.

In writing this book, the author has called on a lifetime's constantly renewed experience of this varied and fascinating country and upon his knowledge of most, if not all, sectors of its human communities with whom he could conduct a dialogue in one of several languages. In some instances he has been bold enough to indicate probabilities, but the geographer may not venture as far along this road as does the roving journalist or the amateur diplomat.

ACKNOWLEDGMENTS

I should like to thank the following for permission to use copyright materials in the construction of maps and diagrams: the Government Printer, Pretoria, Republic of South Africa (Figures 4, 5, and 12); the Editor of *Economic Geography* (Figures 6, 7, 8, and 9).

My thanks go also to: Dr. G. Etzel Pearcy, senior editor of this series, for his valued encouragement and advice throughout the preparation of this manuscript; and to my wife Mary, who deciphered my handwriting, typed the first drafts, and made many wise suggestions.

D.L.N.

Contents

Figures (following p. 88)

Introduction: A Note on Political Entities

With the winds of change in Africa have come many new names of countries, lakes, rivers, and cities. The new names express the justifiable atavistic pride of a new nation. Southern Africa has also experienced some changes, which for clarity's sake should be set down for the reader.

(a) The Republic of South Africa. Originally established as the Union of South Africa in 1910, it became first a Dominion and then, following the Westminster Acts of 1931 and 1934, an independent member of the British Commonwealth. Unwilling at the time to submit to the principle of multiracial equality, South Africa left this growing community of independent nations to become a republic outside the Commonwealth in 1961. A President has replaced the Queen of South Africa as titular head, but little else has changed constitutionally or in parliamentary procedure. The four provinces—the Cape, Transvaal, Orange Free State, and Natal, the colonies which originally came together in 1910—remain separate entities of the republic, having control over a limited number of administrative departments.

(b) The British Protectorates. Three landlocked British territories of Bechuanaland, Basutoland, and Swaziland came into existence in the second half of the nineteenth century in order to preserve them from the Boer republics of the Transvaal and Orange Free State, the land-hungry farmers of the Cape Colony and Natal, and the colonial ambitions of Bismarck and Cecil Rhodes. The Act of Union implied that all three territories should pass to the Union Government after the inhabitants had been consulted. They became known as the British High Commission Territories.

Succeeding British governments, reluctant to make such decisive changes, were even less willing to do so after the Nationalist government came into power in South Africa in 1948. Instead, each territory has been allowed to work its way up the ladder of independence, to become free of British control, and then to make its own decisions about future relationships with its neighbours.

Bechuanaland became Botswana (population 550,000) in 1965; Basutoland was renamed Lesotho in 1966 after it had been granted independent status, choosing a system of limited monarchy with cabinet government, while Swaziland, already freed from protectorate status, was to be granted its independence in 1969. Only the last-named (population 300,000) is in any way economically viable. It has minerals to exploit, forests to cut, and abundant land and water for agriculture of all kinds. Botswana relies on extensive cattle-ranching in a highly vulnerable semidesert environment, but is known to have some useful mineral deposits awaiting exploitation. Lesotho (950,000) farms wool and wheat but is bereft of any resources, except for a small diamond-digging area in the mountains. All three countries export male labor to the Republic, upon which they rely to buy their entire production and to supply most of their technical and veterinary services.

(c) South-West Africa. This ex-German colony became a C-Class Mandate after World War I and was by agreement administered as an integral part of the Union, under the authority of the League of Nations. After World War II the Union would not agree that the United Nations had jurisdiction similar to that of the League; despite many controversies in the General Assembly, the Union has continued to integrate the territory into the Republic. Included in the area is the Caprivi Strip, an interesting geographical relic, designed by the Germans to link South-West Africa with the supposedly navigable Zambezi River. It is now under South African control.

1 *Subtropical Paradise? Removing Some Illusions*

NINETEENTH-CENTURY explorers in Africa—Livingstone, Cameron, Stanley, Peters, and the rest—did a great disservice to the continent by painting its natural resources and potential value for agricultural settlement in extravagantly glowing terms. It has taken a century for men to recover from this euphoria to the point of facing squarely the environmental difficulties: infertile, unrewarding soils; unreliable, inadequate rainfall; plant, animal, and human diseases. Our continuing inability to find quick remedies for these has somewhat tempered the optimism inherited from men who had hoped to convert this continent into a rich food garden for its inhabitants. Illustrated tourist brochures emphasize the advantages of South Africa over most of its tropical neighbors. Unlimited mineral resources have undoubtedly made it the richest country in Africa, able to afford all the luxuries and amenities of a modern industrial state. The unvarying sunshine of the wide open spaces and the unsurpassed assortment of magnificent landscapes offer a perfect vacation for those who can get there. This description is all true; yet at the same time the environmental restraints on the rest of Africa manifest themselves just as readily in the south—drought, hail, floods, inadequate soils, diseases, and pests—all are abundantly evident in the country's past and present agriculture and will doubtless be so in the future. Often there can be no final solution to such problems. People learn to live with them and make the most of the advantages remaining. Only in the second half of this century has the country, at great expense, begun to appreciate and make the most of them.

The Republic of South Africa covers an area of 472,359 square miles, approximately equal to the total area of Texas, Oklahoma, Arkansas, Louisiana, and Mississippi. If South-West Africa is included (317,725 square miles), then Arizona, Nevada, and Utah have to be added for the sake of comparison. The country spans some 14 degrees of latitude, from 22° S to 36° S, and about 16 degrees of longitude, from 17° E to 33° E. There are more than 1,800 miles of coastline with only a few bays or indentations suited to harbor construction. The offshore continental shelf terminates sharply within five miles of the coast, although recent marine explorations along the southern coast have revealed a number of submerged peaks rising within twenty fathoms of the ocean surface. Beyond this, to the south, east, and west there is nothing for several thousand miles but bare ocean dotted with a few barren islands. Most of the shoreline is buffeted by such heavy surf from the Atlantic, Southern, and Indian Oceans' swells that landings by boat are usually impossible.

Two major ocean currents sweep the coast. The Mozambique Current, a warm, south-flowing stream, skirts the entire coast as far as the Cape of Good Hope. Here, it intermingles with a sub-Antarctic water mass which wells up from below the ocean surface near the Cape and flows northward as the cold Benguela Current. Counter-eddies from each add to the dangers along the shore and help to deposit large sandbars at the mouths of most South African rivers.

THE LANDSCAPE

Within strict latitudinal limits, South Africa is subtropical, with only a fraction of its area north of the Tropic of Capricorn and, unlike South America, having no land extending into the "roaring forties." Its peculiar topography, however, takes away most of the subtropical element too, for much of the country lies 4,000 feet above sea level, thus modifying the effects of latitude, virtually creating temperate conditions in all but the coastal fringe, and offering a wider range of bioclimates than usual.

Geological Structure. Geologically, most of South Africa is associated with the African Shield, one of the oldest and most stable of the earth's land masses. Such a history partly explains the absence of great alpine or folded mountain ranges like the Andes or the Rockies, for although there are two slight examples of this mountain-building—an east-west and a north-south belt which meet in the southwest Cape—they are older and worn down and are not as significant as, for example, the Andes in modifying environmental conditions.

The rest of the subcontinent has suffered dimpling and warping as the result of great crustal strains and only in mid-Cretaceous time do we have evidence of a major fracture which set the fragments of Gondwanaland drifting away. By comparison with Europe and North America, South Africa's lithology and geological structure are simple.

Imagine a fairly "heavy" layer cake sitting on an old breadboard. The latter would represent aeons of time covering 2,000 million years, during which a number of geological cycles succeeded each other, involving many thousands of feet of igneous, sedimentary, and metamorphic rocks, heavily modified by folding. Into this was injected a vast granite mass, and the whole was shaved down by erosion to a low level. This was the Basement Complex, rich in minerals including gold and stibnite from the Murchison Ranges and asbestos from Barberton.

In varying proportions our layer cake represents each succeeding geological era, the earliest of which, the pre-Cambrian, covers a period of extended sedimentation in which small particles of gold were deposited to form the Dominion Reef and Witwatersrand systems. From the steeply dipping beds of this great basin, some 75% of the world's gold is mined today. Another ancient basin, about 300 miles in diameter, known as the Bushveld Igneous Complex, dominates the Central Transvaal. Its rim is composed of a series of concentric ridges whose role in determining road and rail routes may be compared with that of the Appalachian Mountains of the United States. Many economic minerals such as chromite, platinum and tin are extracted from the area.

Ensuing cycles of erosion reduced most of these earlier rock systems to a low plain upon which further sediments, some continental, others marine, were laid down. This was the last time that South Africa was invaded by marine seas.

Our attention shifts now to the southern part of the country, where for 350 million years a vast sedimentary basin (geosyncline) slowly deepened as it received increasing loads of sediments, not only from southern Africa but also from much of the surrounding Gondwanaland landmass. These events were terminated by a glacial epoch whose ground moraine, deposited by several continental glaciers, attained a maximum thickness of some 2,000 feet and is known as Dwyka tillite. Much of this has since been eroded away.

The Karroo System, which followed, is world-famous for its fossil reptile remains. Sedimentation continued in the vast intracontinental lake along the edges of which extensive coal beds were laid down. Local folding on the southwestern edge of the geosyncline produced the one and only fold mountain system of the Southern Cape. A gradual change from water-borne sediments to wind-borne sands and dust (the Beaufort and Stormberg Beds in the interior) points to the effectiveness of a rain shadow to the east of this new mountain system, with resultant desiccation.

Vast outpourings of volcanic lavas topped off the underlying, gently dipping sedimentary strata over many thousands of square miles of the country, much in the manner of a chocolate icing on our layer cake. Subsequent cycles of erosion have, however, stripped much of the lava from the present-day landscape. The Drakensberg Escarpment and all the sedimentary beds between its crest (as well as an occasional exposure of the Basement Complex) and the Indian Ocean tell the almost complete history of 2,500 million years of geological succession.

Deposition along the margins of the subcontinent of later marine beds and a few isolated sediments bring the geological history up to date. Apart from a few intrusions of kimberlite (diamond-bearing volcanic pipes), the only major influence on the interior was the insidious expansion of the Kalahari sands, which in the not-so-distant past covered an area extending from the Congo to the Orange River.

Pleistocene climatic fluctuations in South Africa took the form of alternating pluvial and dry phases, reflected in all the major river valleys as terrace gravels, containing datable human artifacts. There can be few areas in the world with a greater proliferation of stone implements dating from the Old Stone Age to the Late Neolithic and Bushman periods.

Much of South Africa's land surface is therefore composed of ancient rocks, on which have been laid a series of continental sediments. All but the narrow coastal plains have been so deeply breached by one cycle of erosion after another that in one place the Basement Complex may be exposed and in another, only 100 miles away, a complete succession of South Africa's geological column may be exposed.

Physiography. Two elements dominate the South African landscape—the Drakensberg Escarpment and the Highveld plateau. Both have been powerful influences in the country's historical development: the Escarpment, a massive erosional scarp retreating towards the interior, demarcates the coastal slopes from the Highveld. Originating in Rhodesia it may be traced near the eastern boundary of the Transvaal, breached by several large rivers, the Limpopo, Olifants, and Crocodile, whose valleys provide air mass entrants on to the Highveld. The Escarpment gradually rises to its highest elevations in northern Natal (where a pass provides a road and a rail route into the Transvaal), Here, it reaches 11,000 feet above sea level in places and offers a steep barrier between Natal and Lesotho, surmountable on foot through narrow defiles. A pioneer trail through Sani Pass can now be used by jeeps.

Further south it declines once more in height and turns further inland through the Suurberg, Sneeuwberg, Nieuwveld, and Komsberg. Turning north as the Roggeveld Mountains and the Bokkeveld Range, it continues through Namaqualand into South-West Africa and finally as far as northern Angola. Everywhere along this section of the Escarpment a major river has cut far into its slopes and in places created the necessary gap for routeways to the interior, used by *veeboer* (stockfarmer) trekker, railroad, and highway.

The interior plateau, between 2,000 and 6,500 feet above sea level, consists of a number of subregions, the most important of which is the Highveld, a plainland 4,000 feet to 6,000 feet above sea level. There is a surprising variety in what appears to be a monotonous landscape. The tips of very ancient rocks are exposed as ridges in the western, central, and southern Transvaal, while southwards across the Orange Free State and Karroo dolerite caps form mesas and buttes on the plains.

Below the Escarpment, there is always a sharp drop through an intermediate landscape to the low coastlands, which seldom attain a width of more than a few miles except in northern Natal and in South-West Africa. In the Cape, two ranges of fold mountains lie between the Escarpment and the coast. One trends east-west and the other south-north. They form a multiple ridge-and-valley landscape, conjoining in the southwest Cape as a complex mountain knot, through which must pass the Great North Road from Cape Town to Johannesburg.

Rivers and Drainage. Lacking a high and dramatic continental watershed like the Rockies or the Andes, South Africa's rivers nonetheless find their way either westward to the Atlantic Ocean or eastward to the Indian Ocean, from the Great Escarpment edge. While the Orange River originates in eastern Lesotho, some 1,300 miles from its Atlantic mouth, only a few hundred yards away from the vertical walls of the eastward-facing scarp, the headwaters of the Tugela gather strength for their run to the Indian Ocean. There are many such streams which flow perennially and tumultuously eastward, cutting down deep valleys and leaving between them long sinuous spurs that peter out near the coast. Further north, other east-flowing rivers such as the Sabi, Limpopo, Olifants, Crocodile, and Pongola have broken through the main scarp and have their headwaters well back in the interior plateau.

In the south and southwest the Cape Folded Mountains have caused the main streams to adopt a trellis drainage pattern; structurally guided into synclinal valleys, they occasionally break through anticlinal ridges before reaching the sea, providing historically important gateways (Afrikaans: *poort*) across difficult country. A number of inland drainage basins, found in the western and northwestern parts of South Africa may become extensive shallow lakes after heavy rains, but they soon dry up.

Of the westward flowing streams, only the Orange River and its major tributaries, the Vaal and the Caledon, are in any way important. For much of its course the Orange is exotic, usually receiving most of its waters from its upper course in Lesotho. The lower tributaries like the Molopo and the Zak are at best intermittent, and during a period of drought even the main stream dries up. A large-scale 30-year project has been initiated in order to use this river basin to the best advantage (pages 129–132).

Unfortunately, most of the east-flowing and south-flowing rivers, usually perennial and fast-flowing, have, with the help of their tributaries, dissected the eastern and southern flanks below the Escarpment into very rough terrain, with slight (if any) usable flood plains. Despite the advantages of permanent water supplies, agriculture is well-nigh impossible in many areas. Other uses are being found however, for this abundant water source (pages 160–161).

WEATHER AND CLIMATE

South Africa does not extend southward beyond 36° S. It lies accordingly wholly within a subtropical climatic regime. Furthermore, it is flanked on three sides by oceanic waters which insulate the country from the sudden winter freezes so characteristic of North America's subtropical regions. The very cold air masses coming out of Antarctica must pass over 2,000 miles of comparatively warm ocean surface and are therefore quickly modified (though still cold) when they reach the Cape.

To the west and east are semipermanent subtropical anticyclones whose circulation feeds the country with a warm maritime air mass. Tropical continental masses settle over it in winter, while in summer equatorial air flows in from the north. Temperate depressions in the "roaring forties" take a winter course which allows their cold fronts to sweep in from the southwest across the entire country, often to be followed by an Antarctic cold front.

Differences of elevation and topography are also a major factor in the local weather and climate. Except for the coastal lands below 1,500 feet, the subcontinent experiences, as a result of elevation, marked temperature anomalies and reduced humidity. On the high plateaus above the Great Escarpment, between 100 and 160 nights with air frost are registered every winter, during quiet anticyclonic weather. Strong temperature inversions and cold air "pools" are also found in the many deep valleys below the Escarpment.

Rainfall. Winter rains and dry summers are characteristic of the southern and southwestern Cape. A narrow belt west of Port Elizabeth receives perennial rainfall. Over the rest of the country winters are dry and rain falls in spring and summer. "Three-day rains" in September or October from the Indian Ocean herald the spring plowing; the convectional summer rains of the high plateaus are often associated with thunder, severe lightning, and occasional heavy hailstorms which cause considerable damage to standing crops and livestock. Flash floods are common in most river valleys in late summer, when storms break over the upper basin of a dry river.

Along the upper flanks of the Drakensberg Escarpment the mean annual rainfall is about 120 inches and is mostly orographic, while on the eastern Natal midlands a "mist" belt is created by the uplift of warm moist Indian Ocean air. Otherwise, mean annual values range from 60 inches on the east to less than one inch on the Atlantic coast. West of the 20-inch isohyet, agriculture and livestock farming become increasingly difficult. More significant, however, is the unreliable and variable nature of the rainfall. Five-year droughts have been experienced on a number of occasions in the past century, affecting every section of the community and causing widespread economic distress. The greater part of the country was drought-stricken between 1929 and 1935 and again from 1960 to 1966. In addition, evaporation rates both in summer and winter are extremely high, making the interior plateau an area of water deficit.

Snow is uncommon and does not lie for long, except along the Drakensberg crest. Lesotho, northern Natal, and the southern Transvaal have all suffered complete isolation from time to time, with extensive livestock losses and (in mountainous areas) human starvation.

Despite the regular daily sunshine and clear cloudless skies, South Africa is not well placed climatically. Most of the total rainfall runs eastward and largely unchecked to the Indian Ocean. The winter rains of the southern and southwestern Cape provide excellent conditions for farming but nowhere else is it possible to rely absolutely on rainwater for agriculture and livestock farming.

The borehole well has enabled livestock ranches to survive over most of the interior plateau. Unfortunately, much borehole wellwater is heavily alkaline or poisonous to man and beast, and where borehole supplies have been possible, the water table has been falling steadily during the past forty years. Out of some 250,000 boreholes, some 25% are dry or yield less than 60 gallons per hour. Much of this decline is linked with increased runoff, veld deterioration, overgrazing, and soil erosion rather than with secular climatic changes.

VEGETATION

As might be expected, the distribution of vegetation in South Africa is closely related to climatic patterns and elevation, with soils usually playing a secondary role. Man's occupation of the area during the past five hundred years has probably brought so many changes that it would be very difficult to describe the original natural vegetation. Forest and bush appear to have been much more widespread than they are today.

Ecologists consider that South Africa represents an area of competition between "Cape" flora, composed of "Mediterranean" plants in the south, and tropical forests, grasslands, and savannas advancing from the north. In the climatically ill-favored marginal area between them is the unique Karroo scrub, comprising the species from both sides which can tolerate such conditions. These are therefore excellent pioneers and colonizers in either direction.

Apart from a narrow strip of tropical mangroves along the Natal coast, most of the eastern flank, before man's intervention, was covered with a thick subtropical forest, most of which has been cleared for agriculture. Further south and on the highest slopes of the Natal Drakensberg, this gave way to temperate evergreen forests occupying areas of perennial rainfall. Remnants have been preserved from total extinction in the George and Knysna districts. These slow-growing forests were renowned for their hardwoods—ironwood for wagon wheels, yellowwood for general timber, sneezewood and stinkwood for old Cape furniture—and were heavily exploited until about 1940, when it was decided they should be conserved.

North of the subtropical forest zone towards the tropics, the lowlands and river valleys were occupied by typical savanna—tall grasses and bushy trees—the environment of most African wild life; and since it was excellent grazing land, this region was subject to many changes by burning and abuse.

Within the southwestern Cape area, a highly specialized chaparral-like vegetation, able to withstand dry summers, has survived throughout centuries, despite the ease with which it can be ignited. Its major representative shrub is the *Protea,* the national flower of the country.

On the high plateaus, South African vegetation becomes predominantly grassland or *veld*. Tree growth is inhibited by the dry and frosty conditions. Two well-separated types of grass—short "sweet" varieties in the east and taller mixed varieties towards the west—may be identified. These were both suited to grazing, since each thrived at a different season, but heavy regular burning, particularly before all vegetative growth had ceased in the sweet grass, has altered the entire ecological structure of these natural grasslands. They have also been invaded by Karroo pioneers as far north as the southern Transvaal. Most of the *veld* areas suffer serious phosphorus deficiencies resulting in botulism among grazing animals. Restoring these grasslands to their original vigor is a matter of general policy in all the *veld* areas of the country.

Further west, grass veld or tall grass savanna yields to Karroo bush and scrub, consisting of sparsely distributed varieties of fleshy succulents and thorny low scrub. Cattle give way to sheep and ultimately to goats, especially in overgrazed areas. On the west coast true desert conditions prevail.

SOILS

As a result of the country's geological history most of the South African soils are "green" or skeletal. Under a poor vegetation cover, and with high evaporation, they lack the humus of more temperate soils. There is, for example, only one small area of the bushveld which resembles the chernozems (black earths) of the American plains. Quite extensive laterization occurs in the moister regions, and in the Natal midlands a ferricrete band some two to four feet thick is found at or near the surface.

Since most of the soils are residual, the fragmented particles are angular. They tend to compact after rain, encouraging runoff and soil erosion. There are likewise few alluvial areas of any size except along the Caledon and Vaal-Hartz river bottoms as well as parts of the lower Orange. The Transvaal lowveld however has excellent soils for irrigation farming.

Unfortunately for South Africa, neither white nor black farmer learned early enough to nurse these difficult soils; apart from a tendency to erode naturally, they have been abused, almost to a point of no return. Considerable sums are being spent on their rehabilitation (pages 21–22).

DISEASE

Although malaria and yellow fever were endemic in northern Natal, in the Transvaal lowveld, and along a number of valley bottoms, they have been steadily eliminated and no longer present a danger to human health. Tsetse fly was prevalent in northern Natal and Zululand but, using aerial spraying, the central government has been able to drive it out of South Africa. Only one major endemic disease offers any real difficulty. Bilharzia (schistosomiasis) a debilitating snail-borne disease passes via infected water to human beings. Irrigation agriculture unfortunately encourages it to spread so that its distribution area is on the increase in the lowveld.

ENVIRONMENTAL HAZARDS

When all the physical, edaphic, and ecological elements of the South African landscape are compared, it is clear that there are many more unfavorable features than favorable. Without the backing of mineral wealth which can be taxed, it would long since have ceased to possess a viable farming economy. In order to maintain a rural agricultural population, successive central governments have resorted to subsidies, price supports, and other financial devices. These have in part kept inefficient white rural communities practicing maize growing and pastoral farming according to the traditional ways of their forefathers on marginal lands which should have been abandoned long ago. It should be realized, however, that even the most efficient farmer cannot fight destructive natural hazards and that he too requires subsidy if food is to be grown for the whole country.

Ironically, the largest section of the population, the tribal Bantu, occupy lands which are the most favored. Between Natal and the southeastern Cape, great stretches of high-quality arable and grazing land normally receive adequate rainfall, abundant sunshine, and little frost. For many generations little more than subsistence farming has been practiced in the reservations. Government policy ruled out any form of compulsory improvement, so that until recently, overpopulation, overstocking, deforestation, lack of contour cultivation, and many other causes reduced such areas to great poverty. At the same time the white farmer in the Natal midlands or East Griqualand showed that wheat, maize, mutton and woolled sheep, dairy products, and vegetables could, under identical ecological conditions, be successfully grown.

It has been shown that only 15% of South Africa's agricultural lands are arable. What is more important is that 70% of that fraction lies east of and below the Great Escarpment. In order to make the best use of these arable areas, it has been realized that the Bantu tribal reservations will have to be rehabilitated and converted to an efficient cash-crop economy as soon as possible. Experiments have shown that they are capable of producing large surpluses of grains and beef, for sale to the rest of the country. In no sense should these lands be considered marginal (as is frequently implied, mainly for political ends). To the geographer it also seems doubtful to argue that 80% of the people own 13% of the land if no weight is attached to the quality of the land. The plea for more land made by Chief Luthuli in his book *Let My People Go* would have greater validity if the kind of land he wanted were available—land for an abundance of richly fed cattle and many virgin acres whose surface could be raped for maize. Converting present-day rural slums to economically active farming areas is the only choice left for those who live east of the Escarpment. In some regions such as the Transkei (pages 159–160), it is already happening.

West of the Escarpment there is abundant evidence that except for a few favored regions, farming is at best a marginal occupation. Many thousands of white families, in the face of increasing environmental difficulties, have abandoned their rural heritage in favor of the city. Water shortages, droughts, the withering crops in the field, dying stock, the approaching dust storm, and the menacing sight of locust swarms were familiar features to all those who lived through the first half of the twentieth century in this part of South Africa.

Like the American Dust Bowl, much of this plateau country was best suited to stock raising and, therefore, to have plowed it for maize and sorghum brought its sorry reward. Much of the topsoil of the Orange Free State, northern Cape, and western Transvaal has been blown away by the dry winds of winter and spring when the rains failed to arrive on schedule. Even stockmen who confined themselves to rearing cattle and sheep found the grasslands deteriorating, after years of indiscriminate burning, to scrub thornland and clumpy sour grasses. Soil erosion followed in the train of such primitive techniques.

Since the passage of the 1946 Conservation Act, one of the most comprehensive of its kind, serious attempts have been made to halt the destruction of the soil. Nearly 90% of the white farming areas of South Africa have been declared conservation areas, subject to rules controlling land use and conservation of resources. Only recently, however, have further steps been taken to reduce the number of Bantu squatters and other low-wage labor, in an attempt to modernize farming techniques, to reduce subsidies, and to rationalize landholdings—reinforcing what nature has been doing for some time. Bantu tribal communities, reluctant to change their ways or to reduce their livestock numbers, have only recently begun to accept soil conservation as a first step toward modernizing their economy. Their problem, exacerbated by the absence of thousands of young men working as migratory laborers in the gold mines and industry, will only be gradually solved, since only demonstration and voluntary persuasion can be used.

Apart from drought and soil erosion, all farming communities have stoically to endure such unenviable and costly risks as hail, lightning, and flood. There are, of course, other elements which they can turn to their favor. Mineral fertilizers are now used in rapidly increasing amounts to overcome soil deficiencies. Irrigation farming, long practiced in the Great Fish, Vaal-Hartz, and Lower Orange valleys, has rapidly spread to the Transvaal lowveld, Natal, and the Transkei and is revolutionizing food production. Grassland management programs—using such excellent indigenous grasses as Pangola (*Digitaria decumbens*) and Red Grass (*Themeda triandra*)—fencing, pasture rotation, and controlled burning are being carried out by White and Bantu alike.

The most outstanding transformation, however, in the South African rural landscape during the past two decades has been the result of widespread forestry programs both in the private and government sectors. Although eucalyptus gum plantations (for mine pit props) and wattle plantations (for tanning extract and rough timber) were cultivated, it was considered as late as 1939 that the country would always be a net importer of timber products, including paper. Conservation forests, initially for watershed protection, proved so successful that plantations of fast-growing pine, salignum, and poplar now cover most areas suitable for silviculture. South Africa is now self-sufficient in paper pulp, most softwood timbers, and processed hardboards. Bantu tribal areas have also become forest-conscious, not only to meet fuel and building demands but also to provide raw materials for local furniture manufacture and prefabricated housing.

Keeping animal diseases at bay has always been a part of South African farming life. Regular arsenical dipping of all livestock to reduce the risk of east coast fever through tick infestation, and immunization against rinderpest and anthrax, were both the direct outcome of veterinary research carried out in South Africa. Though resented, particularly by Bantu cattle herders, quarantine against these diseases and particularly against foot-and-mouth disease, have been strictly applied throughout the country at great expense. It has therefore been possible to preserve much of the subcontinent's livestock from complete annihilation.

In summary, there are many natural hazards built into the South African environment; little can be done to overcome them. Those who have tried to adjust themselves have generally failed to meet the challenge. Other equally serious difficulties have proved capable of solution by costly outlay of time and money. The latter has proved the easier to obtain; the former is critical, and whether it is too late for the country to recover its slight but valuable agricultural lands from complete destruction will not be known for many years to come.

2 *The Peoples of South Africa*

ONE reason for South Africa's current notoriety among the nations of the world is the policy of *apartheid*. This is an Afrikaans word, commonly interpreted as racial segregation, and roughly equated by most people with the patterns of socio-economic separation of Negro ex-slaves from white men in many states of the United States. It is, however, an analogy which, when closely analyzed, is more apparent than real, and though it may at times have been politically expedient to ignore the discrepancies, it is important to understand that they exist and are rooted in history.

The Bantu nations were never enslaved; although defeated in battle, they were not decimated to a point of extinction and have not, even in industrialized societies, wholly discarded their strong tribal fealties, their different language and customs. This should surely be enough to differentiate them from the rootless American Negro communities, forced by circumstances into using the English language and losing all contact with their native Africa. Only recently has world opinion come face to face with the reality of tribal nationalism and what damage it can wreak within the borders of most African countries south of the Sahara, despite their racial homogeneity as Negroes.

What is often forgotten, when South African racial issues are raised in this way, is the fact that it is not simply a question of the Bantu Negro helot oppressed by his white overlord. The ethnic make-up of the South African population is more complex than this oversimplification would indicate. Nuances of color, physiognomy, religion, and race dictate socioeconomic stratification and mobility throughout the country, and so-called "racial" prejudices have more commonly disguised a fundamental conflict between ethnic groups in overt competition for an assured place on the economic ladder, particularly in rural areas and among the ranks of unskilled labor. There are a number of such marginal rivalries which involve not only white and black but all the variegations from Malagasi to Mussulman.

The Five Major Groupings. There are present in South Africa today:

(a) The Khoisan speaking tribes, survivors of the earliest inhabitants of the subcontinent—counted in thousands but no longer in danger of extinction.

(b) A number of Bantu "nations" (tribal groupings with linguistic and cultural affinities), numbering some 12 million people.

(c) The White peoples, about 3¾ million in number, comprising the major groups identifiable as "Afrikaans speaking" (about 65%) and "English speaking" (35%) respectively. Included in these white groups are smaller, long-established clusters whose home language is German. Recent European immigrants from Holland, Belgium, West Germany, and Portugal do not appear to retain their mother tongue for long but are rapidly absorbed into the English-speaking or the Afrikaans-speaking sections. Migrants from the United Kingdom, Australia, and the ex-British countries of Africa gravitate naturally towards English-speaking communities, though there are exceptions who prefer to learn Afrikaans as quickly as possible.

(d) The Cape Coloured and Malay peoples, totaling one and three quarters of a million, the product of three centuries of cross breeding between a great variety of people.

(e) The Asiatic communities, about half a million in strength, and consisting mainly of East Indians from many sectors of Indian life, together with a few Chinese and Arabs.

Added to the ethnic labyrinth is a further complication of uneven distribution not only of the total population but of its segments, some of which are heavily concentrated in one area, mainly as a result of historical circumstances. The general picture, however, shows a strong preference for the eastern flanks of the country. In order to explain such a pattern, it is essential to have some idea of each group's origins and history. After that, it will be possible to comment on population growth and on demographic trends.

THE KHOISAN-SPEAKING PEOPLES

There are three separate peoples to be considered in this group—the Bushmen, the Hottentot, and the Bergdamara. Each is distinctive, yet belongs within a larger family by virtue of many similarities in cultural as well as racial characteristics. All share a vital Khoisan element in their speech—the use of implosive consonants or "clicks." The Bushman and Bergdamara are hunters and gatherers, while the Hottentot is a pastoral herder of fat-tailed sheep, goats, and long-horned cattle.

Many ethnologists consider all three peoples to be derived from a common Bushmanoid stock, whose physical properties are well known—small, symmetrical bodies, steatopygia, and a readily recognized skull structure. The Hottentot, adopting livestock from the southwestern Bantu, thrived under improved diets of milk and meat and in time grew physically taller than the Bushman. Strong negroid characteristics in the Bergdamara present a riddle for which a number of answers have been suggested but none satisfies the skeptic ethnologist.

The Bushman represents our last contact with prehistory. Bush skulls have been located in strong association with refined stone flake spearheads and axes. The descendants of these Stone Age men were relatively abundant throughout east, central, and southern Africa, hunting game with bow and poisoned arrow and gathering nuts, insects, fruit, and wild greens, leaving behind their lively cave paintings and rock engravings. Driven southward by the gradual advance of Bantu-speaking invaders, they were trapped in the Cape cul-de-sac, only to be attacked in the rear by the white settlers of Table Bay. While fair numbers of them were captured and apprenticed as laborers, many thousands were slaughtered by Hottentot and White, like so many vermin.

Retreat through the mountains and finally to the relative safety of the Kalahari Desert allowed the remnants to survive into the twentieth century and even to thrive as serfs of the Tswana or as independent tribes near the Okavango Delta. Groups in South-West Africa have, under tutelage, begun to learn the art of cultivating maize, while others have been employed in diamond mines for their superb eyesight and ability to pick out rough gems. It is uncertain how many "pure" Bushmen survive. In the course of time most tribes have mated with Bantu and particularly with mixed Hottentot slaves who migrated from the Cape settlements in the late seventeenth century. It is not unlikely that the Bushman will eventually emerge from his desert fastnesses and gradually settle permanently near the Orange River as a cultivator and cattle herder. In the latter occupation he had an excellent reputation among the stock farmers of the Cape during the eighteenth century for his ability to use natural pastures to the best advantage.

The Hottentots. The history of the Hottentot peoples differs markedly from that of the Bushmen. They were the first to trade with the garrison of the Dutch East India Company in Table Bay, exchanging livestock for goods. Some of the tribes, however, such as the Korana, the Grigriqua, and the Gonaqua in the southwest Cape preferred to migrate eastward and northward away from this pernicious influence and found peace in the interior. Here they made a temporary home until the white man, also seeking new pastures for his stock, caught up with them. Others such as the Nama, long established in what is modern South-West Africa, lived a purely pastoral life, troubled only by the aggressive Herero and later the Oorlams, a mixed group who, merging with the Nama, spent much of the nineteenth century actively opposing Herero imperialism.

Those who remained behind in the southern Cape were rapidly absorbed as laborers, herders, and gardeners, or if female, shared the beds not only of their masters but also of the masters' slaves. (On occasion they were enrolled as mounted and foot soldiers both against the Bushmen and in Kaffraria against the southern Nguni.) A desperate weakness for liquor, three major smallpox epidemics, and a general breakdown in moral fiber decimated the Hottentots as a group, so that it would be difficult today to find even a fragment of the original strain.

They exist however in many thousands, mixed with white blood, not only in the southwestern Cape but also in Namaqualand, South-West Africa, Griqualand West (near Kimberley), and Griqualand East. Many South African Whites today carry traces of this aboriginal inheritance. The Cape Coloured peoples, more than any other, however, are living evidence of the considerable racial intermixtures of the seventeenth, eighteenth and nineteenth centuries (see pages 40–45).

Hottentots were the object of special attention from various missionary societies during the early nineteenth century, and many attempts were made to rehabilitate them morally and economically by establishing freehold land settlements on which they could farm. Ordinance 50 of 1828, a well-known law freeing them from serfdom in the Cape Colony, enabled large numbers to apply for these lands. Unfortunately, within a generation, most were left destitute from bankruptcy or after exchanging lands for alcohol. Most returned to their labors in the vineyard.

The Bergdamara. Of the Bergdamara, little need be said. Numbering some 45,000, they occupy scattered areas of South-West Africa. Oppressed and enslaved by the Herero and Nama tribes for several centuries, they were unable to maintain a unified grouping. They speak Nama, the language of one of their overlords. Since their emancipation a large number have come under Christian missionary influence and have been absorbed in mining and other industries in South-West Africa. They remain an ethnic enigma.

THE BANTU NATIONS

Among the societies of negroid Africa, those speaking languages whose common root is ur-Bantu have exerted a powerful influence over much of the sub-Saharan continent. From their hearth, located in all likelihood east of the Niger River in West Africa, these people went eastward and southward, mingling with other differentiated groups in violent combat or peaceful contact. The full history of the Bantu-speaking peoples and their migrations has not yet been told, and only if we are extremely lucky in our archeological findings will it ever be known or reconstructed.

Linguistic studies have provided some of the answers. For example, contact with a Khoisan-speaking people is often indicated by the inclusion of one or more of the five major "click" sounds. Zulu, Xhosa and certain Sotho dialects make use of at least three clicks in their speech. Cultural evidence such as kinship and political organizations, pottery, ironwork, beadwork, and other material techniques have offered evidence of absorption of one group by another. In the absence of written records, oral traditions have also provided a hazy if not entirely reliable background which, when supplemented by rare Portuguese and Arab archival data, offers some ideas about the origin of the Bantu of Southern Africa.

Bantu Migrations. All linguistic research demonstrates that the Bantu are but a branch of the Nigritic peoples in West Africa located somewhere near the Cameroon Highlands. Their major territorial expansion began some 1,900 years ago, through tropical rainforests on to the savannas and grasslands of East Africa (with the exception of the southwestern Bantu of Angola and South-West Africa who may well have pursued an independent route southwards).

Certain sections of these Bantu ventured into the southern cul-de-sac of the continent and by 1450 A.D. were scattered along the well-watered lands of the southeastern seaboard. (This is confirmed by recent evidence, derived from Portuguese archival records, which shows that shipwrecked Portuguese mariners some 60 to 70 years later were received by the communities.) To these most southerly Bantu, whom we have specifically named *Nguni,* the next five hundred years were to bring expansion and conquest, internecine warfare, power, and finally, subjugation at the hands of white armies.

Those people called *Sotho* represent the ultimate southward surge of this great Bantu wave. They began to arrive on the central high-veld about 1700, gradually spreading during the following century as far west as Bechuanaland (Botswana) and as far east as the edge of the Great Escarpment—at this stage a very effective migration barrier between the Sotho and Nguni-speaking nations.

Classifying the Southern Bantu. On various ethnographic and cultural grounds all three major groups of the southern Bantu may be subdivided as follows:

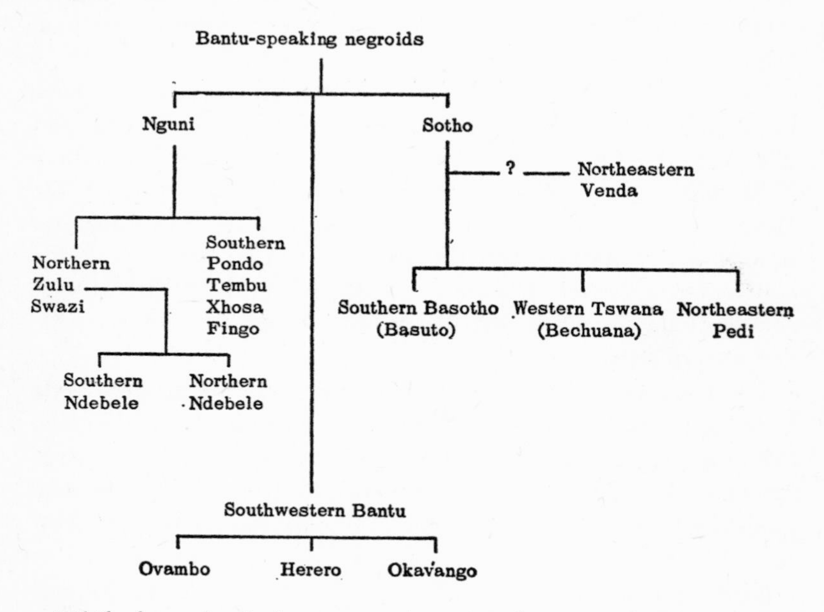

While for polemical purposes these peoples may simply be called "Africans" or "Bantu," they display a number of differences in organization, culture, and economic activities which make it necessary to discuss them in detail.

All share the root Bantu language, although this does not imply that there is mutual comprehension within the various language subgroupings. As with the remainder of negroid Africa, the problem of communication becomes paramount where men of numerous tribes are drawn together, for example in the Zambia copper mines or the Johannesburg gold mines. Choosing a *lingua franca*—Swahili, English, Portuguese, French, or even an artificially created simplified language such as "Fanakalo"—has proved to be the only solution, despite the fact that nine out of ten of the workers are Bantu.

The mother tongue offers little in the way of a unifying force.

Physically, the Southern Bantu have all the traits of the negroid race, although distinct variations can be measured in skull morphology and skin color. These have come about as the result of intermixing with Khoisan and Hamitic peoples during the long migration from the hearth.

The Mixed Economy. Major changes in diet and crops must have accompanied the traverse from tropical rainforest to savanna and grasslands, but much of the evidence for this remains conjectural. What is certain, however, is that somewhere in East Africa the Bantu assimilated from the Nilotic peoples the techniques of pastoral nomadism which, combined in greater or lesser degree with the cultivation of cereals such as maize, sorghum, and millet as well as other food crops, provided the mixed economies so characteristic of Southern Africa.

These admixtures have had considerable influence on the mode of life of the Bantu nations. Where pastoralism played a major role, the males devoted much of their energy to cattle keeping while females cultivated the land. Such division of labor has only very gradually been modified under the changing conditions of modern life.

Cattle in Bantu Life. Horned cattle played an indispensable role in the social structure of Bantu society. They were the equivalent of the bank balance, representing by numbers, colors, horns, and shape the status of an individual in society. They provided milk, but were killed only on ritual and festive occasions. The results of this excessive devotion to livestock are reflected in the overstocking, poor quality scrub cattle, overgrazed pastures, and extensive soil erosion of most Bantu rural areas.

Cattle have generally been an important part of Bantu marriage formalities. The so-called bride price, an incorrect interpretation or the Zulu "lobola," consisting of a negotiated number of animals, was handed over by a man to his prospective parents-in-law, representing in part an insurance against the bride's fertility and fidelity. Despite many attacks on the custom by young males, it survives even in the sophisticated Bantu urbanized communities. All that has changed is the nature of "lobola" itself, which today may be hard cash, leather, saddlework, or similar goods.

Horticulture. Cultivation, practiced somewhat haphazardly, solely by women, provided cereal foods (and therefore beer) for everybody and was supplemented by wild fruits, greens, and game. Increasing populations within restricted reservations did not modify local custom to any extent, so that women have continued to ignore contour hoeing, crop rotation, and fertilizers, greatly to the detriment of crop yields and conservation.

Given the complete freedom to wander slowly southwards and then to return north from the Cape cul-de-sac, the Bantu could have continued to survive with a mixed economy. Unfortunately, the white man, engaged in identical practices, interposed himself between the Bantu and their destiny.

Social and Cultural Organization. Social organization among the southern Bantu was generally patrilineal and centered upon the *tribe,* the head of which was the *chief.* His authority was partially limited by the male heads of a central nucleus of families who were considered to be the founders of the tribe. To the chief fell the responsibility for allocating arable land and pasture lands, initiating fertility and harvest rites and making decisions which reflected the tribal consensus. In a world of self-determination and universal franchise, it is all too often forgotten that such philosophies run counter to tribal practices, which are the product of centuries of wielding a delicate balance of power, yet producing just as valid a result as from any other system.

Bantu society also accepted polygyny, thus enlarging a simple kinship system into one of extended family relationships which bewildered monogamous-minded laymen and missionaries when they saw it in action. Children, especially boys, were seen as the principal purposes of marriage; and since the mothers were ranked in seniority within the kraal, complex questions of inheritance had to be set down. To this had to be added age groups, who, outside the family relationship, went through puberty and manhood initiations together, thus forming life-long bonds of fraternity.

All Southern Bantu believed in a Supreme Being, but they worshipped their ancestor spirits who were thought to be all around them in daily life. Fortune and disaster were associated with the mood of these ancestors. Consequently, a belief in magic, good and evil, and sorcery can still be found even among Christianized communities, who prefer to keep a foot in both camps. It may be essential to them, for example, to explain to the factory foreman that you can no longer work at a particular machine because your grandfather's ancestral spirit is sitting on it. Magic in fact, with the help of a witch doctor, is more than ever a part of Bantu industrial workers' lives today, and large sums are spent on medicine (*imuthi*) which will cause the factory manager to smile upon his men and so "make their day." Practitioners are frequently called in to exorcise unhappy spirits which have infected buildings, houses, or rooms with their presence (*intakathi*). Murder and homicide cases in law courts are commonly attributed by the accused to the baleful influence of a little hairy being, *Thikoloshe* or *uHili,* whose actions forced them to such an act. These aspects of Bantu spiritual life cannot be lightly discarded or ruled *ultra vires*.

Until scholars interested themselves in the subject, Bantu tribal law was unwritten. It rested upon tradition and precedent. Few sights were more impressive than a gathering of elders to decide upon a criminal or civil offense against society or alleged breaches of contract. The young were educated in tribal law from an early stage in their lives so that, when adult, they were presumed to know the laws as well as the consequences if transgressed. Lawyers, legal historians, and anthropologists in southern Africa have successfully recorded most of these for use in the country's law courts, where it is possible for Roman-Dutch and various forms of native law to differ from each other in application.

Within Bantu tribal society there were thus general similarities which in sum were probably greater than the differences. Yet the latter should not be dismissed as irrelevancies in any South African situation. Once a man is fully urbanized or away from tribal authority for considerable periods, such differences tend to disappear, but it must not be assumed that this will automatically take place. On the other hand, attempts by various local government authorities to maintain tribal barriers within a single Bantu township have only been partially successful. All too often it is human nature which disturbs the pattern, when Swazi seeks Tswana and Xhosa woos Sotho.

The Nguni Tribes and Offshoots. It is unfortunate, too, that romantic novelists and historians have portrayed the Bantu peoples chiefly through the history of one nation—the northern Nguni, better known today as the Zulu—whose warring activities in the nineteenth century rippled outwards from their homeland until they were felt as far north as the East African Lakes region. A stereotype was established and persists well into the present day of a giant warrior whose word, like the Englishman's, was his bond. Should a white South African be asked to name the Bantu nations in his order of preference, most commonly it will be the Zulu who comes out first. In view of the legends, this is not surprising.

Preliminary attempts by Dingiswayo, king of the Mthethwa to unify the Natal Nguni in the early decades of the nineteenth century provided his successor, Shaka, with an excellent military organization for conquest and expansion. From disparate scattered clans an entire nation was welded. The males underwent a truly Spartan preparation for war, while a system of attack based on a crescent moon formation was reinforced by a change from the thrown spear (*assegai*) to the shorter stabbing spear.

During Shaka's paramountcy, most of modern Natal and Zululand was laid waste as part of a scorched earth policy; clan after clan was subjugated and many thousands of refugees were driven southward and westward by superbly disciplined foot regiments whose main task was to bring back cattle as loot. Malcontents and refugees led their armies away from Natal to establish their kingdoms elsewhere. Mzilikazi, one of Shaka's lieutenants, after rampaging through the modern Transvaal, ultimately made his home across the Limpopo in Matabeleland. Soshangane, head of the Ndwandwe, moved northward into Gasaland (west of Lourenco Marques) dominated the local Tonga, and became known as king of the Shangana (Shangaan). Zwangendaba, chief of the Ongoni, with his army, swept northward as far as the Rift Valley lakes in one of the bloodiest sweeps of all, well remembered by many tribes even today. They ultimately settled on both sides of Lake Nyasa and are generally known as the Angoni.

By driving their enemies outward and away from the Zulu heartland, Shaka's regiments also disturbed other Bantu groups, and in particular the tribes of the Southern Sotho who had gradually populated the area of modern Lesotho (formerly Basutoland). The Tlokwa (Batlokoa), under their queen Mantatisi, adopted a similar belligerent policy by sweeping westward and southward and destroying all who stood in their way, until they were stopped by the Tswana.

All in all, the period 1815–1850 was a savage phase in the history of the Bantu people. It is to this day called *Mfecane* (the crushing). Missionaries, explorers, and nomadic stockfarmers from the Cape observed not only the total destruction wrought by these tyrants but also the breakdown of all organized tribal life. With this in mind, it becomes possible to understand why the Voortrekkers (1834–1845) had such a comparatively easy passage in their own northward migration from the Cape to the Vaal and beyond.

Shaka saw little reason to object to the presence of white men on lands near Durban where he had carried out his scorched earth policy. Thus, the first English colonists were able to live in complete accord with the tyrant, whose successor, Dingane failed, however, to keep up friendly relations. Dingane, in fact, responded to the presence of the first Boer Voortrekkers by slaughtering them all during a meeting on December 16, 1838, at which land grants were being discussed. This incident has been enshrined in South African history; and although Dingane has the sympathies of some scholars of the period, it proved to be a foolish and provocative act which could only lead to the destruction of the Zulu nation, first by Boer riflemen and ultimately in 1879 by British artillery.

The modern Swazi nation of Swaziland is also Nguni in origin. A number of clans, first under Sobhuza and later under Swazi, subjugated or drove off the resident Sotho and made themselves masters of the country. Similarly the genius of Moshoeshoe (Moshesh), with the help of defensible mountain terrain, enabled the southern Sotho not only to resist the Zulu regiments but also to bring together from every part of the interior large numbers of refugees, all of whom were welded into the Basuto nation.

Finally, the increasing pressure placed on the frontiers of the Southeast Cape by these violent forays reactivated the border conflicts between Boer and southern Nguni, which resulted ultimately in firm British intervention and the restrictions of various tribes to certain specified areas or reserves, in which traditional tribal law and custom held sway for more than a century. Each Bantu nation (except the Basuto under Moshesh) submitted to white force of arms during the second half of the nineteenth century and found itself in a reservation which gradually represented the original homeland, under the then prevailing conditions, with enough land for all the inhabitants.

The twentieth century however, has brought many changes to the Bantu nations in their reserves. Rapidly growing numbers both of people and of livestock have led to the remorseless destruction of lands. Increasing contacts with mines, the town, industry, the farm, and the factory have caused many able-bodied men and women to abandon their reserves for a better life in the cities. Much of South African political action during the past ten years has been aimed at rehabilitating the Reserves and reversing the trend.

THE WHITE PEOPLES

Early History. In 1652 about fifty years after the colonization of Virginia, the first white man stepped ashore in Table Bay, in order to establish a small victualing garrison for ships of the Dutch East India Company. Portuguese mariners had always avoided this southern coast, in view of the hostile reception they had faced from local tribes in the last decades of the fifteenth century. They collected fresh water under heavy protection and were always glad to be back on board. Only by accident was it made patent that the Cape milieu was ideal for settlement when the crew of an "Indiaman" was shipwrecked in 1648, yet successfully survived until rescued a year later. Seeds and plants from the wreck thrived, and cordial relations established with local Hottentots made fresh meat readily available.

Jan van Riebeek, a loyal servant of the Company, gave up ten years when he should have been accumulating a personal fortune in the Indies so that as Governor he could get the station on its feet. His small garrison of 400 men, Dutchmen and mercenaries of every European nationality, became the country's first permanent settlers—if we ignore the unknown numbers of Portuguese sailors who in the early part of the sixteenth century survived shipwrecks on the rocky shores of Algoa Bay and went native.

The changes of population and official personnel transfers from the Indies to the Netherlands have not been fully explored by archivists, but it is clear that Table Bay very soon became a desirable station. Despite the Company's intentions, it also became impossible to hold the garrison within certain restricted boundaries. Eight years after its founding, the Cape had ceased to be a station and had become a colonial settlement, without the complications of charter or plantation status which were used in North America and in the West Indies. From then on, the South African frontier expanded without interruption eastward and northward for 250 years. It was in fact a process analogous with the expansion of the interior frontier of North America. The most important decision of this decade 1652–1662 was one which allowed the importation of slaves. It immediately changed the nature of the settlement and greatly contributed to its permanence (pages 40–43).

Small in number but powerful in their influence, a number of Huguenot immigrants from La Rochelle and other Protestant areas of France were brought to the Cape by van Riebeek's successor, Simon van der Stel. They were quickly integrated with the predominantly Dutch farmers and were forced to abandon their French tongue and any thought of a cohesive group. The Huguenots brought two features to the Cape—the vineyard and deciduous fruit on the one hand, and on the other, a plethora of French surnames such as Du Toit, Du Plessis, Malherbe—the only relics in modern South Africa, save for a few words in the Afrikaans language, of an illustrious past. Of some interest is the fact that, coming from the north of France, the Huguenots did not bring the olive tree with them, and this product was unsuccessful in "Mediterranean" South Africa until this last decade.

A steady accretion of settlers in the Cape took place throughout the next century. It is safe to assume that the great majority came from Holland and from Germany and that by 1750 there were about 5,000 colonists and 6,000 slaves.

English Immigration. British purchase and annexation of the Cape in 1815, after some years of occupation during the Napoleonic wars, brought the next major influx to the Colony. The soldiers and administrators were relatively isolated from the Dutch pastoralists, and it was not until 1820 that a serious attempt was made to colonize parts of the southeastern Cape with English immigrants under the 1820 Settlers Scheme. Some 5,000 were settled in the hinterland of Algoa Bay (Port Elizabeth), mainly to form a buffer between the Dutch and Bantu pastoralists. Though many succeeded as farmers in this frontier zone, a large number reverted to their former skills and crafts in rapidly developing urban communities.

Further injections of English immigrants also occurred in Natal between 1849 and 1851 under the Byrne Settlement Scheme, whose main aim once again was to convert unemployed, industrialized Englishmen into active farmer-settlers. The growth of Durban and Pietermaritzburg seduced large numbers of these folk away to town life. Sir George Grey, a Cape Governor, brought some 12,000 English and German settlers to the country between 1857 and 1862, generally with the same result—a quick migration to the nearest town. It is therefore easy to account for the pattern of white settlement in South Africa during most of the nineteenth and twentieth centuries—the Dutch as farmers and pastoralists, and the English as craftsmen, tradesmen, and professionals in the small but rapidly growing towns.

The discovery of diamonds in 1867 followed by that of gold (1886) on the Highveld led to an agglomeration of nationals—Australians, Americans, Englishmen, and Central Europeans, all seeking a quick fortune. Extracting coal from northern Natal became the monopoly of Cornishmen, Welshmen, and some Scots. All added to the strength of the English-speaking communities, concentrated in the mining towns of the Witwatersrand, Kimberley, and Natal.

Later Migrations. A little noticed but significant growth of German settlements in the second half of the nineteenth century also left its mark on the landscape through names such as New Hanover, Wartburg, and others in Natal. Place names observed on a large-scale map of South Africa offer an excellent demonstration of this population mixture.

Much of the great, continuous migration from Europe which was to benefit North America, Australia, and New Zealand bypassed South Africa, as did the benefits of the European Industrial Revolution. Many attribute this fact to the presence of cheap ex-slave and black labor. More likely to blame was the erroneous image of a savage jungle occupied by cannibals and carnivores, current in much of the evangelist literature of the time and which persists even today among some Americans. It was enough, in any case, to discourage immigration.

During the twentieth century there have been sporadic waves of immigration particularly from the United Kingdom, Holland, and Germany, none of which was enough to alter the basic ratios of English and Dutch (by this time sufficiently deviant from the original to be called Afrikaans) speakers. Since World War II, in strong competition with Canada, Australia, and New Zealand, the South African government has been combing Europe for suitably qualified immigrants. British, Greek, Italian, German, Dutch, and Portuguese applicants are now arriving at the rate of some 40,000 per annum. As in Australia, these are likely to remain outside the mainstream as "new" South Africans, but they will ultimately exert a powerful demographic and religious influence.

Equally important is the growing rate of intermarriage between English speakers and Afrikaans speakers, especially in the larger towns into which the rural Afrikaner has flowed during the past twenty-five years. Although the demarcation line remains in the countryside, it has become increasingly blurred even in "English"

Natal—not without some unfavorable reaction from the conservative elders of both sectors.

THE CAPE COLOURED COMMUNITY

Origins. The term "coloured" has a specific connotation in South Africa and should not be confused with the meaning loosely given to it, particularly in the United States. Thus, the Coloured, "Cape Coloureds," or *bruinmense* (in Afrikaans) are not simply Negro or the result of cross-breeding between white and negroid Bantu peoples. They are in part a complex, wide-ranging intermixture of peoples from East Asia, India, Madagascar (modern Malagasy Republic), Angola, and Mozambique. All were brought to the Cape as slaves by the Dutch East India Company from 1659 onwards and mixed with local Hottentot and Bushmen communities, white settlers, soldiers, and sailors. Thus, the "coloured" community is in essence one of the most complete racial and ethnic blends in the history of modern man.

In order to prove ancient lineage (in this situation, about 150 years of continuous residence), most white families in the country claim a "coloured" ancestor, unlike the pure Castilian families of the Argentine, for instance, who proudly boast their pure Spanish blood and absence of Indian admixture. An observer of the South Africa scene frequently encounters, for example, the nickname "Swartie" (Blackie) applied to Afrikaans-speaking whites in all spheres of political and social activity. While a few of these may derive from a negroid Bantu strain, most reflect the adaptability of settlers of the seventeenth, eighteenth, and nineteenth centuries to a world without white women in the Cape. Even under strict mid-twentieth-century legalistic taboos, the process continues, evidenced by regular appearances in court of white offenders against the Immorality Amendment Act of 1950, which forbids sex relations between whites and nonwhites.

Slavery and Miscegenation. In many respects, slavery as an institution ran a very different course in the Cape from that of North America and the West Indies. Jan van Riebeek's dilemma as first governor proved to be one not only of curbing his garrison within its fixed boundaries but also of finding manual labor. The vanguard Bantu tribes, it must be emphasized, were some 500 miles to the east and did not become available as labor for another 150 years; the only local people, the Khoisan-speaking Hottentot and Bushman tribes, failed to volunteer their services. Other contemporary transatlantic colonists bought imported West African slaves, but after a sickly experimental shipload from this source had been delivered to Table Bay in 1658, van Riebeek preferred to turn eastward for his labor. Java and Madagascar provided the first wave. The latter became the principal area, thus compounding the ethnic confusion, since the inhabitants of that island, although negroid, showed clear evidence of admixtures from Indonesia, not only in their physical characteristics but also in cultural elements. Malagasy, an Indonesian tongue with some Bantoid remnants, was the principal language. There are also records of slave purchases from the Mozambique coast of Bantu-speaking Negroes known locally in Afrikaans as "Masbiekers."

The decision to import slaves from these various sources is generally acknowledged to have been one of the most powerful factors influencing the subsequent development of South Africa. Failure later to attact white settlers in large numbers—peasant laborers and manual workers—from Europe, for instance, is attributed to the presence of slave populations. It is unfair, however, to compare this trend with the all-white population growth in Australia and New Zealand nearly two centuries later, where the economic hardships that the European proletariat at that time experienced played a decisive role. Nonetheless, for South Africa the presence of slaves altered the character of settlement and exploitation as they had originally been planned by the Company.

By 1750 there were, working in Cape Town and in the vineyards and wheat farms of the Southwestern Cape, well over 6,000 slaves living among about the same number of free men. In this way arose the master-servant relationship between the white and nonwhite very much along the lines of the plantations of the West Indies, which is held by some to account for the arrogant race attitudes of some modern Afrikaners to manual labor, though this theory is not corroborated by observation of the fruit farmers of the southwest Cape, a conspicuously liberal and race-tolerant community.

English abolition of the slave trade in 1807 resulted in an immediate reduction of incoming eastern slaves, although contraband cargoes occasionally slipped through the naval blockade. Thereafter, the only addition to the population from this source were the so-called "prize negroes," landed from British men-of-war which removed them from slave ships in mid-Atlantic. Such men were apprenticed to local government employers (or local private citizens) for periods not exceeding 14 years. It is important to realize that between 1808 and 1816, the period of greatest naval vigilance in the Atlantic, some 2,000 of these people were landed in Table Bay. Mostly from the Gold Coast, they further added to the ethnic complexity of the local nonwhite population. Among other minor groups of this type were the Free Blacks, descendants of the Company's oriental political prisoners or their entourages. The Free Black probably represents the classical stereotype of the Cape Coloured of Cape Town, for he was, like many of the Indonesian slaves, a Muslim. He was also a skilled craftsman, tradesman, fisherman, and smallholder. His descendants are today largely Muslim and successfully pursue those trades, particularly in greater Cape Town. They vary widely in skin color and physiognomy but are unified into the Cape "Malays" by their singular devotion to Islam. Against the grey teutonism of Calvinist Afrikanerdom, their colorful festivals and parades provide a unique example of spontaneous gaiety.

Abolition of Slavery at the Cape. For most slaves, emancipation represented only a minor change of status. From 1795 until 1838 they were increasingly treated as a valuable commodity and were permitted to earn money through their skills (enough in a number of instances to buy manumission), the men by making furniture or building wagons, and the women by sewing. Large numbers left their owners after release, to swell the populations of a number of mission stations such as the Kat River Settlement, Philippolis, and Genadendal. Equally large numbers remained behind to take their place in urban Cape Town as skilled craftsmen and gardeners.

Their language was Dutch and English (since they had no other), their religions Mohammedan, Protestant (particularly Dutch Reformed), and Roman Catholic. Within a generation they had acquired franchise in the Cape Colonial responsible government (1853).

Until their growing strength on the common electoral roll in the southwest Cape forced the Nationalist Government to rescind this status (entrenched in the Act of Union of 1910) in 1956, the Coloured peoples in the Cape were held in social esteem and permitted a social freedom of action rarely encountered in other parts of the country. Their artistic abilities in music, opera, and dancing particularly, were early recognized, and traditional skills of both men and women were effectively used in the furniture, textile, and other industries. In rural areas, on the other hand, the vineyard and fruit orchard retained large numbers of Cape Coloured families, which, tied by the "tot" system (a daily free allowance of alcoholic liquor such as raw brandy), have not made the same progress. Other Cape Coloureds dominate the important inshore fishing industry of the Cape peninsula and have the virtual monopoly of the vegetable and flower production of urban areas not only in Cape Town but in other towns of the Republic. Not a few have entered government service and are employed nationally in the postal and railroad services.

Nonetheless, the Cape Coloured communities (despite the considerable progress in housing, welfare, and education provided for them) have of all the ethnic groups been the most deeply offended by racial separation in the Cape since the advent of the National Government in 1948. They have failed to advance in many areas where it had been assumed that multiracial attitudes would prevail. As the buffer between white and Bantu, they may yet play an important part in providing skills which are today so scarce throughout the country.

The Hottentot as Slave and Freeman. The imported slave was not the only wellspring of miscegenation. Khoisan-speaking Hottentots, nomadic pastoralists loosely organized into a number of tribes, bartered their fat-tailed sheep and humped cattle (ancestors of the famous Afrikander cattle) for liquor, metal, and trinkets. Some of these, repelled by the presence of the white man, migrated into the empty lands of the north and northeast, hoping in vain to escape. Others, lingering within range of the Dutch settlements, though not enslaved, were quickly reduced to peonage and squatter status by allowing their lands to pass to enterprising Dutch farmers for a trifle. The latter prized the Hottentot as a herder and shepherd, though not as an agricultural laborer. Not until Ordinance 50 was passed in 1828 were these Hottentots able to escape the very severe restrictions placed on their movements.

The Basters. A predominantly male slave population was encouraged to find mates among the Hottentots, thus producing another racial mixture. White settlers also chose Hottentot women for concubines and occasionally married them. From this crossbreeding process emerged the *Basters* (Afrikaans for bastards) whose descendants, led by patriarchal leaders such as Adam Kok and Barend Barends, migrated northwards and northwestward from the Cape to become separately identified communities. They carried with them into isolation their white genes, their Calvinist dogmas, and the Cape Dutch dialect. The wanderings of the Basters into remote corners, their contacts with Hottentot tribes which had fled the Cape a century before, and their eventual disintegration under severe pressures from acquisitive White colonists competing for the same grazing lands—these are today part of South African frontier history. Many gathered about the stations of the London Missionary Society or the Moravians in what came to be called Griqualand West, and East Griqualand (in the neighborhood of modern Kokstad).

The best-known Baster group to survive intact crossed the Orange River between 1868 and 1870 and settled in an area which was soon to be claimed by Germany as a colony. Named the Rehoboth Basters, some 12,000 descendants today occupy the Rehoboth Gebied in South-West Africa. Governing themselves through traditional patriarchal laws, the Basters have developed within their community a strong class structure and employ considerable numbers of Damara and Hottentot to perform all their menial labor.

Minor contributors to this grand *melange* were the Bushmen. Harried and slaughtered in thousands by Hottentot, Baster, and white settlers, they and their children were regularly captured and handed out as apprentices to farmers, who regarded them as highly trustworthy herdsmen and undoubtedly encouraged them to settle down with Hottentot and slaves.

It must be stressed that apart from the influx of "prize" negroes, there was little of this kind of contact with the Bantu. The true "mulatto" population of South Africa is rare and comparatively recent in origin, coming after a great part of the country had been settled. English colonists, explorers, missionaries, and miners were just as responsible for their appearance as the migrating Boer farmer.

ASIAN PEOPLES

The Chinese Coolie Experiment. Smallest in numbers among the four ethnic groupings, the Asians are represented by East Indians originally from the Indian subcontinent (some 500,000) and scattered Chinese families found chiefly in Johannesburg and other major cities and totaling some few hundreds. The presence of Chinese in South Africa was the direct consequence of a shortage of Bantu labor in the Witwatersrand gold mines immediately after the Anglo-Boer War (1899–1902). Searching for adequate substitutes, the Transvaal Chamber of Mines began to import Chinese coolies (mostly through Canton). By 1906 this exotic element totaled some 52,000. Unfortunately, as a labor force they did not prove amenable to mine and compound discipline and in the face of considerable violence among the Chinese themselves, the employers began shipping them back home. By 1910 only a small number remained in Johannesburg, and these settled down into the traditional trades of laundryman, grocer, or gardener, the only remnants of a potential fifth ethnic group, whose presence and treatment in South Africa were enough to turn out a British government in 1906.

Indian Indentured Labor. The East Indians, on the other hand, have a longer ancestry than the Chinese. The Colony of Natal took advantage of a world trend following the abolition of slavery

(1838) in British colonies, when sugar-growing countries sought indentured agricultural laborers from India. As a direct result, countries such as Trinidad, Guyana, Fiji, Mauritius, and even temporarily Australia received large numbers of "coolies" to overcome their agrarian labor crisis. Natal settlers (including Mauritian French cane-growers), unable to attract Bantu men, who regarded agriculture as women's work, therefore looked to India to supply manual workers. The Indian government, having seen the sorry effects of this policy elsewhere, grudgingly signed an agreement in 1859 allowing the export of coolie labor. The latter (including a proportion of women) were entitled to free return passages, a three-year indenture, two further years of free choice of employer, and a grant of Crown land should the return passage not be taken up. These conditions varied from time to time, depending on the state of the sugar industry and on the Indian government's attitudes, but from the available evidence it is clear that few Indians opted to return to their homeland. On the lands granted to them they rapidly developed a horticulture, maize, and tobacco cultivation so successfully that by 1900 they dominated large areas as well as smaller towns in coastal Natal. They spread rapidly, too, into the coal-mining industry and railroads as firemen and maintenance men, and into the hotels and restaurants as waiters. Although some set up shop as small traders, it was left to later waves of merchant immigrants from Gujerat to make the considerable advance which is so evident today in cities such as Durban.

Once again, the presence in Natal of an exotic population such as the East Indian was complicated by the variety of origins, castes, customs, languages, and religions so characteristic of the Indian subcontinent itself. Among those responsible for the education of the young Indian, the prospect of having to provide five separate languages within a school system to allow for religious vagaries and social customs, or to modernize Indian attitudes towards females, would surely daunt even the bravest.

Indian Communities in Other Areas of South Africa. Rapid population growth, particularly in Natal, under improved health and welfare, declining infant mortality, and longer life expectation have brought remarkable changes to the Indian communities. Muslim and non-Muslim live in amity; English has become the *lingua franca,* and India has ceased to be the motherland for people who are now fourth-generation South Africans. Urbanization and absorption in manufacturing industries have also divorced most of the younger generation from the sugar canefields where, ironically, the rural Bantu is found to be the ideal worker as well as owner-grower. There are many prosperous Indians, particularly in the import-export business, in textiles, and in clothing and furniture industries, so that in the urban areas of the Transvaal, Natal, and the coastal Cape, a major class structure, only slightly complicated by religious and caste differences, has evolved.

The Indian in South African Politics. The political history of the Indian in South Africa since 1860 is equally complex. It is not generally known, for instance, that when freed from his indentures, he was completely unrestricted in his choice of schools for his children and (under property qualifications or a minimum wage-earning capacity) he possessed full adult franchise until its withdrawal in 1896. Growing opposition among white colonists to Indian competition in all spheres of economic life, and penetration of residential areas, resulted in many restrictions.

Trading licenses, immigration permits, and increased pressures for compulsory return to India of all Indian labor became the staples of Natal politics. The Orange Free State had from its inception refused to allow Indians to reside within its borders, while the Transvaal conducted a policy of laissez-faire, despite available restrictive legislation, mainly on grounds that these aliens were highly skilled as traders and therefore useful to the community. It was in this growing atmosphere of hostility that Mahatma Gandhi between 1894 and 1913 conducted a long-drawn-out legal battle on behalf of local Indian rights. Although he won a number of concessions, Gandhi failed to reduce the powerful prejudices which gradually build up against Indians wherever they settle.

The Indian government continued to seek to improve the lot of the alien Indian in South Africa by establishing his property and citizen rights. A protracted struggle between Nehru and Smuts came to a climax in one of the earliest sessions of the General Assembly of the United Nations (1946). Since that date, India has pursued a relentless opposition to South African domestic racial policies and provided the rallying point for all Afro-Asian nations.

Within the Indian community, miscegenation is comparatively rare, although there are a number of instances of Bantu-Indian and White-Indian cross-breeding. On the other hand, intermixture within the group has been accelerated by the disintegration of caste as a divisive force, the increasing use of English and Afrikaans, and a phenomenal rise in school attendance and in technical and professional education.

3 *Population Distribution and Demographic Trends*

THE TOTAL population of the Republic of South Africa was estimated on June 30, 1966, to be 18,298,000, an increase of slightly less than 2½ millions over the total of the last official census held in May 1960 (15,841,128). There were in 1966: 12,465,-000 Bantu, 3,481,000 Whites, 1,805,000 Coloureds, and 547,000 Asiatics.

All totals, except that of the Bantu, are considered to be reliable, since they are based on reasonable long-term records of vital statistics. Although census figures for the Bantu population are becoming more reliable, vital statistical data remain very weak, for it was only in 1952 that compulsory registration of births and deaths became law. The major difficulties have otherwise been the association of head-counting with hut taxes and the remoteness of many areas. The presence within the republic of more than one million migrants from other African countries, some having entered legally and others having slipped across the frontiers in search of work, has further complicated the process. Demographers have therefore to exercise great caution in estimating the future growth of the Bantu nations.

FACTORS AFFECTING POPULATION DISTRIBUTION

In terms of simple densities, South Africa averages 39 persons per square mile (compared with 11.0 in 1904), an overall figure which is valueless for all practical purposes of comparison. It fails to convey the reality of the present-day population distributions as well as the accelerated pace of areal changes during the twentieth century.

Water Availability. More than two-thirds of South Africa's population is located in the eastern third of the country and along the southern coastal flanks of the Cape Province. This eccentricity is easily explained. The remaining western two-thirds is too dry to support anything but extensive pastoral herding, particularly of hardy sheep and goats. For a number of reasons it is not easy to define physically the eastern and southern limit of this low-density area (less than five persons per square mile). Annual rainfall fluctuates widely, severe droughts are common, evaporation is high, and heavy frosts are frequently recorded during the winter. Furthermore, with the advance of Karroo vegetation engendered not by climatic change but by man himself, the ecoboundary between steppe and grassland is also on the move. Most authorities therefore tentatively place it between the 16-inch and the 24-inch mean annual isohyets, and until the Orange River Project (pages 129–132) and kindred schemes have been completed, population densities westward to the Atlantic are bound to remain very low and even to decline as more and more borehole wells dry up. Farther east, the Drakensberg Escarpment, whose tundralike summit plateaus and precipitous eastern flanks do not invite settlement, has often been a haven for refugees in the distant past; but today it lacks many permanent inhabitants, so that population densities along this zone are also very low. Scattered communities occupying this vital watershed area have, in fact, for conservation purposes been persuaded to move away in the past 20 years to lower areas, thus reducing the total population almost to zero. Extensive wild game preserves, e.g., Kruger Park (8,000 square miles) are also devoid of significant populations.

Diseases. On the other hand, endemic diseases such as malaria, yellow fever, and sleeping sickness (trypanosomiasis), confined to the eastern coastal belt and river gaps in the Eastern Transvaal Escarpment, did not limit settlement as they have done further north. The Nguni tribes in Natal, however, always chose whenever possible to live on the long, winding spurs which separate the eastward-flowing rivers on their way to the Indian Ocean, in order to avoid the miasmas (malaria) and temperature inversions of the valley floors. Such ribbon patterns of population distribution are just as persistant today in rural Natal and Zululand.

Location of Settlements. By contrast, a river ford or a reliable water supply was the chief factor in the growth of white settlements in the eighteenth and nineteenth centuries. Many villages and small towns evolved near a river ford, the focus for all wagon trains, and today as a result of such locations suffer the disadvantages of inversion "smog" as they develop and industrialize. When nomadic stockmen and the Voortrekkers, in their journeys across the highveld, came upon springs flowing out of Karroo dolerite sills, they generally gave the subsequent camping site a name which ended in "fontein," e.g., Bloemfontein, Bultfontein.

White and Other Migrations. Because the eastern third of the country was favored with good spring and summer rains, it was inevitable that two migratory groups, both of whom coveted the excellent grass pastures for their cattle, should come into conflict in this zone. All the events which followed this clash between White and Bantu pastoral nomads dictated in large part future settlement patterns everywhere from the eastern Cape to the northern Transvaal. It accounts for the halting and stabilization of the Southern Nguni in Kaffraria, in the Transkei, and in Pondoland. In search of their rural Utopias, the Voortrekkers forsook this eastern passage and took instead a northward route much farther to the west of this tribal block.

In order to protect their grassland pastures, the Zulu nation pitted themselves against those Trekkers who branched eastward into Natal from this westerly route. In the face of this resistance and of the presence of British forces, the Voortrekkers retreated from the coastal strip of Natal, which soon became an English colonial settlement.

It is interesting to compare the history of northward migrations from the Cape to the west of the 20-inch isohyet. Hottentot and Baster tribes, struggling to maintain themselves in so hostile a milieu, broke down very quickly or were driven farther into the Kalahari wilderness, where today small clusters of their descendants barely eke out a living. Lacking the water and grass of the eastern side of the country, their pastoral economy could not survive the rigors of frequent drought or the isolation of distance from a market.

Mining and Industry. Mining of diamonds, of gold, and of coal, which followed in quick succession after about 1870, probably exerted more influence on the distribution of population of the entire country than any other factor. A chain reaction started in Kimberley (diamonds) and spread to the Witwatersrand (gold) and later into northern Natal (coal), attracting many thousands to the mining areas. Towns grew up around them and seaports were established along the coast, all of which ultimately became the industrial manufacturing cities of today. Rural depopulation not only rudely disrupted the mixed-cattle economies of both White and Bantu but at the same time caused a vast human tide to flow to cities which were ill-prepared to receive it.

Urbanization. Most countries, advanced and developing alike, have suffered the blight of irreversible, accelerating urbanization. South Africa is no exception. The past fifty years have witnessed an astonishing change in rural/urban ratios not only in the total populations but also in the individual ethnic groups. Abandoned farms on the *platteland* (rural farming areas) and broken-down tribal reserves are both mute evidence of this change. Urbanization as a descriptive term is difficult to apply equally to all ethnic groups in the country. The English immigrants from 1820 to the present day were industrial urbanites, and most remained that way. The rural Afrikaners have only urbanized since about 1930—first as refugees from the stark poverty of their fragmented farms, taking any available town job, however lowly, and secondly as mining and industrial workers in the post-World-War-II expansion period. The Bantu and Asiatic Indians have come to the town via several routes, while many Cape Coloured, privileged in their skills and craftsmanship as slaves, took these with them into emancipation in 1834 and immediately fitted into the mold of urban life in the Cape Peninsula.

It is therefore necessary to examine each individual group's progress from country to city piecemeal rather than as a total population. The basic facts of urbanization are, however, plain to see (Table 1).

Table 1

Urban Population of South Africa

Year	*Total Urban*	*Urban % of Total Pop.*	*Bantu Total Urban*	*U. %*	*White Total Urban*	*U. %*	*Cape Coloured Total Urban*	*U. %*	*Asiatic Total Urban*	*U. %*
1904	1,222		361		599		219		44	
1911	1,546	24.7	526	12.6	677	51.6	265		80	
1921	1,950	27.9	658	14.0	908	59.6	286	51.9	99	60.7
1936	3,218	32.4	1,252	18.4	1,367	68.0	446	56.9	153	70.8
1946	4,482	38.4	1,902	23.7	1,793	74.5	580	60.9	208	71.3
1951	5,494	42.6	2,391	27.2	2,089	78.5	731	64.7	285	77.5
1960	7,481	46.4	3,471	34.6	2,582	83.6	1,031	68.7	397	83.5

Sources: Statistical Year Book 1965 and *Union Statistics for Fifty Years 1910–1960.*

POPULATION PROJECTIONS

The population of South Africa in 1904 was 5,174,827. By 1966 it had been more than trebled, growing at a steady rate throughout the 62 years, and faltering only momentarily after the Spanish influenza pandemic of 1918–1920. If a range of annual increase between 2.1% and 2.5% is used, then South Africa may expect to have between 37 million and 42 million by the year 2000. It is not considered that immigration will contribute significantly to this growth, which will result from a natural increase of more than 2% per annum.

In common with other developing countries, South Africa is therefore facing a population "explosion," resulting from a moderately high birth rate, declining death rates, and infant mortality, combined with longer life expectations. Reduction of all forms of morbidity is the result of improved medical and welfare facilities, better housing, feeding, and education, as well as the elimination of wars and pestilence.

While this summation is generally true of the country as a whole, can it be applied to each ethnic group?

THE KHOISAN-SPEAKING PEOPLES

Surviving elements of the Bushman and Hottentot tribes are still numerous enough to be counted, despite their location in the marginal wildernesses of southern Africa. Most have, however, intermingled with neighboring Bantu, making it impossible to distinguish so-called "pure" strains.

Experts such as Philip Tobias have stated that there are only twenty Bushmen living today in their home area, the Cape Province. There is also a small group living near Lake Chrissie in the southeastern Transvaal. In recent years, however, several scientific expeditions into remote parts of the subcontinent have shown that Bushmen survive in far greater numbers than had been suspected. Instead of a conservative 6,000, the total has now been raised to at least 55,000, of whom some 30,000 are to be found in Botswana. The remainder are in South-West Africa (12,000) Angola, Rhodesia, Zambia, and of course, South Africa. Their demographic vigor has apparently been grossly underestimated, and any assumption that the Bushmen face total extinction needs some revising.

It has already been shown that many Hottentots, in making a considerable genetic contribution to the Cape Coloured People, ensured that they would be remembered for centuries to come. Others were able to escape helotry while still relatively homogeneous but have unfortunately long since become extinct. The Nama of South-West Africa, numbering some 35,000, have been able to survive without much difficulty as the sole representative of a once widespread nomadic pastoralist community. Close contact with the Khoisan-speaking negroid Bergdamara (45,000) makes it impossible to assert any demographic conclusions about the Nama. Since they are also regarded as excellent workers, they are drawn to the town, where they soon lose their identity.

THE BANTU

Absence of Statistics. Little can be said with any certainty about the demographic characteristics of the Bantu. Of the 12½ millions in 1966, 29% were Xhosa, 25% Zulu, 17% Southern Sotho, 10% Western Sotho and 9% Northern Sotho. The remaining fractions were Swazi, Ndebele, Shangana-Tsonga, and Bavenda. From sample surveys it has been calculated that Bantu birth rates are between 43 and 47 per thousand, but with crude death rates estimated to be between 27 and 32 per thousand, the natural rate of increase of the Bantu is only 15 per thousand. The Bantu net reproduction rate, an important index of future growth, is 1.45. The masculinity ratio among Bantu of 104.2 has remained consistently well above 100, mainly because most foreign immigrants are male and therefore load the scales. If the latter are excluded, this ratio falls to 95.5.

The Bantu community is demographically "youthful." Nearly 42% of its population is under 15 years of age and therefore "dependent"—a trend which is likely to persist during the next few decades despite a growing interest in family planning on the part of Bantu parents and the establishment of clinics.

Bantu Urbanization. The most significant statistics concern urbanization and its concomitant rural depopulation. The first country-wide census of 1904 revealed that only 10.4% of the Bantu were living in urban areas. This value had risen to 27% (2,312,000) by 1951 and in 1960 reached 32% (3,471,233)—a value, incidentally, which is regarded as an underestimation in view of the high degree of unlicensed and therefore unrecorded movement to the towns which is known to take place. Despite all attempts on the part of the central government to discourage the movement from the country to major metropolitan areas, it is likely to continue unabated for at least another twenty years. The natural rate of increase among urban Bantu will, during the same period, offset any reverse flow back to the country.

If the Bantu is urbanizing so rapidly, the effects should be manifest in the rural areas and reserves. We must be careful, however, to distinguish between the temporary and the permanent moves for those who go from the country to the mines as migrant laborers on contract are at least economically active, but leave behind their dependents both old and young. The effect on agriculture has been devastating, and although the migrants who return do bring money and goods back from the city, they seldom play their full part in the fields, that is to say, by ploughing, sowing, and reaping the crops for their families. Much of this kind of work is still left to the women, whose fecundity, let it be said, does not decline under such a system of migratory labor. All the wives of the kraal continue to bear children. For obvious reasons, infant mortality is far higher in such rural areas, but there is no evidence of any decline in birth rates. It is within these reserves and other rural areas that the demographic pressures have built up for the Bantu. How best to reduce them is a problem not confined to South Africa.

Secondly, those Bantu who in the past 25 years have been absorbed into the burgeoning industries of the South African cities may have started out as "migrant" laborers, but within a very short time became "stabilized," sent for their families (or married in town) and seldom returned to the kraal. They created the shanty towns and slums, particularly between 1940 and 1946, when wartime production required a vast expansion of the unskilled labor force. The shanty towns have been demolished, but the now urbanized Bantu remain, bearing children who are barely aware of the tribal life their fathers knew.

Future Bantu Populations. It has been estimated that by the year 2000 there will be between 25,000,000 and 28,000,000 Bantu living in South Africa, a total far in excess of the extrapolations offered by the Tomlinson Commission in 1955. What percentage of this population will be urbanized? If we take examples from other countries which have gone further along the road to urbanization, it will be more than 15,000,000, probably located in four or five major cities.

Central government policy is designed, partly through control of movement into the cities, to realize self-government for the Bantu nations (page 157) and border industrial development (pp. 163–66) to make conditions so attractive in the various tribal homelands that large numbers of these permanently urbanized people will voluntarily return to them (page 163). If such a policy should succeed, it will have done what Russians, Chinese, and several other nations have failed to accomplish even by the most ruthless methods. For the dispassionate observer of the South African scene, such a program must prove to be one of the twentieth century's interesting features. Will the present slight movement of some thousands of Bantu families continue to increase with time?

THE WHITES

If treated as a single unit, the white people of South Africa have been well categorized for demographic analysis. There are enough sophisticated statistics in the census and registry records to indicate, as accurately as projections will allow, the general trends of population movement for the next thirty years. Unfortunately, a complicating factor entering into such a discussion is the clear subdivision of the white community into English-speaking and Afrikaans-speaking groups. Although this is but a cultural schism, it nonetheless has biological implications.

Demographic Characteristics. As a single group totaling little more than 3 million, the Whites show some of the characteristics of an aging population. Very low death rates and slowly declining birth rates reveal a remarkably stable demograpic situation (Table 2). Natural increase has been little affected by immigration, although a rapid increase to 40,000 per annum in 1965 and 1966, if continued for several more years, may boost the figures slightly. Infant mortality has shown a marked decline from 67 per thousand live births in 1930 to 27 in 1962. Life expectation at birth for white males is 65 years and for females 70 years, compared with 56 and 59 respectively in 1920–22. The net reproduction rate is 1.54, only slightly higher than the Bantu (1.45), while the masculinity ratio, falling slowly during the past fifty years as a result of male immigration, stands today at 101.4. If the total white population is to maintain its demographic strength, birth rates and immigration will have to rise markedly during the next few decades.

TABLE 2

Vital Statistics of White Population

(per 1,000 Whites)

	1956	*1957*	*1958*	*1959*	*1960*	*1961*	*1962*	*1963*	*1964*
Crude birth rates	24.2	24.8	24.5	24.8	25.0	25.0	24.5	24.1	24.0
Crude death rates	8.6	8.5	8.6	8.7	8.6	8.8	9.0	9.2	9.0
Natural increase	15.6	16.3	15.9	16.1	16.4	16.2	15.5	14.9	15.0

Sources: Statistical Year Book 1965; Union Statistics for Fifty Years 1910–1960; et al.

Projections. At present rates of growth the white population is expected by 2000 to reach 6 million (at 2.1% annual increase) or 7 million (at 2.5% annual increase) and will represent about 16.5% of the total population. Even if large numbers of immigrants alter the present trend, this fraction is unlikely to rise above 20% to 25% in the remaining 33 years of this century. A mass movement on the scale of the great nineteenth-century immigrations to the United States of America also seems unlikely from a Europe which is economically stabilized and politically content. If we consider that in 1921 the ratio of non-Whites to Whites was 3.6 to 1 and in 1960 4.2 to 1, then a value of more than 5 to 1 will have to be envisaged for the year 2000.

The English Sector. Apart from a small number of Cape colonial families, "English" South Africans are either descended from urban-artisan South African stock or came to urban areas during the country's mining-industrial revolution (1904–1967) from urban industrial areas of the United Kingdom. Their demographic pattern of growth was similar to that of pre-World-War-II western Europe (including the United Kingdom)—declining birth rates, lower mortality rates, and aging of population with greater life expectations. Those readers who were students between 1935 and 1938 will recall the gloomy prognostications about the fate of the European and North American populations. The marked increase in wartime and postwar birth rates experienced in England, France, and the United States was reflected only slightly in this section of the South African population, and although immigration from the United Kingdom continues to raise the numbers of "English" South Africans, it has not been enough to offset the decline in birth rates.

The English-speaking communities are therefore demographically destined for a kind of extinction unless a marked change of attitude towards larger families occurs in the next decade. This will not be an obvious extinction, however. Larger forces are fortunately at work reducing the role of language as a divisive element in the community; marriage, business relationships, and political realignments are slowly welding a single white community and reducing the stress of age-old rivalries.

The Afrikaans Sector. There have been several influences in the lives of Afrikaans-speaking communities to make them demographically stronger than the "English." They start immediately with a numerical advantage of 2 to 1. The predominantly rural farming Afrikaner has for generations been inspired by his fundamental faith to beget children much in the manner of the Israelites of old, so that he might be strong in the face of his enemies. In such a patriarchal society, too, sons were highly valued. His churches, as active participants in the struggle for national identity, encouraged him to breed.

Secondly, the Afrikaners belonged to a proud people's army which fought its battles for independence from a metropolitan power some 66 years ago. The nationalistic spirit which emerged from this period has not yet been quenched. It called for more and more Afrikaners to eliminate the English imperialist influence, so deeply resented. To have a large family was therefore to show oneself a patriot. With the coming of republican status, however, in 1961, some of this nationalistic chauvinism has disappeared. Other influences such as urbanization are beginning to exert themselves on the now prosperous Afrikaans city dweller, whose church has often lost his soul, and whose house cannot accommodate innumerable children requiring a full education to fit them for the modern world.

Home Languages. There is no easy way to make a statistical comparison of these trends. Even the use of home language recorded in the census offers but a barely perceptible clue (Table 3). In view of

TABLE 3

Home Languages of White People in South Africa

	1936	*1951*	*1960*
Total	2,003,857	2,641,689	3,088,492
Afrikaans	1,120,770 (56%)	1,502,861 (57%)	1,790,988 (58%)
English	783,071 (39%)	1,039,270 (38%)	1,150,738 (37%)
Bilingual, other European languages	50,411	38,011	44,866

Source: Statistical Year Book 1965.

the sensitive part played by the two official languages in the country's politics and educational system, it would be risky to predict the rate at which one language is absorbing the other. There is, for example, a body of Afrikaans scholars deeply concerned about the way in which *their* language has been tainted by anglicisms, English-derived colloquialisms, and technical terms. Sophisticated Afrikaners do not hesitate in conversation to use an English phrase to convey an exact meaning which would be clumsy or long-winded in Afrikaans.

Along the sidewalks of the traditionally "English" cities such as Durban, Afrikaans is now heard very frequently. It is evidence not merely of the "up-country" visitor to the coastal resorts but also of the rapid rate of urbanization of rural Afrikaners, deliberately transferred to "English" areas by government services or attracted to manufacturing industries. Such towns now possess a number of Dutch Reformed Churches and many Afrikaans-medium schools —all symbols of a rapidly changing population pattern.

Rural Depopulation. The changes in the population pattern have not been happily received in all quarters. Many deplore the sustained loss of Afrikaners from the land from which, according to the national myth, the Afrikaner people draw their moral and spiritual strength. An important government Blue Book, *Report of the Commission of Enquiry into Occupancy of the Rural Areas* (1959) spelled out the serious consequences of such massive rural depopulation, particularly cases of abandoned farms left in charge of nonwhite managers or taken over by squatters. The marginal areas west of the twenty-inch isohyet were most affected.

The Commission was able to show how these losses were affecting the traditional communities of the *platteland* (rural areas). Decreasing numbers of children less than 14 years old and increasing numbers of old people (65 and more), an increasing preponderance of males (against the national trend), and marriage by males at a much later age than in the city all affect demographic aging. Comparative studies of various vital statistics—birth rate, death rate, infant mortality, fertility—showed that the *platteland* sector, the most fertile portion of the white population was becoming "a progressively decreasing percentage of the population." Between 1921 and 1951, the *platteland* lost 405,200 persons to the towns at the average rate of 13,500 per annum. There is abundant census evidence that this has continued at a greatly accelerated pace in the past fifteen years, converting the rural Afrikaner within a generation to a city-dweller.

A sample survey by the Commission also showed that these migrants favored certain types of employment. Sixty-five percent of the police recruits, 40% of the Iscor Steel employees, and 16% of the South African Railways recruits came from the *platteland,* creating yet another group of stereotypes—the raw, unlettered, underprivileged policeman, the ignorant railroad ganger who didn't know why he tapped the wheels of the passing train with his hammer, and the tough uncompromising steel worker willing to destroy his job for the sake of racial supremacy—all of which are reasonably meaningful, yet, like most caricatures, must be modified with the passing of time.

Redistribution of Rural Populations. It is not without significance that the Orange River Project (pages 129–132), a vast development scheme, is directly concerned with rehabilitating agriculture through electrification, irrigation, intensive cropping, and livestock maintenance, not only to ensure greatly increased food supplies but also to restore a vital rural section of the population to the land. Again, this is not a unique South African problem. The United States, England, and France, with very advanced economies, have all witnessed a similar flight by the past generation of farmers and have welcomed the process. South Africa's problem is, however, accentuated by the fact that similar movements of rural Bantu have plunged the host cities into desperate confusion. Nevertheless, it should be noted that for every Bantu man who came to reside in or near the city between 1951 and 1961, some 20 white men arrived too. Can the white man be persuaded, too, to return to his "homeland" in the northern Cape and to practice modern farming? The answer lies in the three decades to come.

THE CAPE COLOURED COMMUNITY

The demographic virility of the Coloured people eliminates any lingering fallacies about the dangers of racial admixtures. They offer an excellent example of widespread genetic absorption without ill effects on their cultural growth. For some white South Africans, on the other hand, holding firmly to the myths of "racial purity," they appear to be living proof of the dangers of racial mixing. Often shorter, thinner, and with a less strong physique than either Bantu or White, in the eyes of a country which is obsessed with sport and the active outdoor life and which worships the human body, they are considered to be physically degenerate. This opinion fails to take into account the fact that many of the group's forebears were small-framed, and that several generations of economic deprivation have not helped to increase their size. But erroneous though it may be, it illustrates one facet of the racial dogma which still bedevils South Africa.

When freed from slavery in 1834, the Coloureds, already well-mixed genetically, were uniquely situated. They were all living within the boundaries of the Cape Colony, and especially in the southwest, were working either as farm laborers or as skilled craftsmen. Even before Emancipation they were allowed to take extra jobs, sell vegetables, or offer their skills in town. Once free, they quickly settled down as a separate community, identifying themselves with Afrikaans or English cultural patterns through language and religion. The population has been regularly augmented by fresh white genes through casual illicit unions; to a lesser degree, it has lost many of its lighter-skinned members who were able to "pass for white."

Emancipation and After. Between 1834 and 1838, all Cape slaves were released. By 1904 the Cape Coloured community had increased to 444,991, of whom 394,864 lived in the Cape Colony. According to the 1960 census, there were 1,509,258, of whom 1,330,089 were residents of the Cape Province. Latest estimates in 1966 indicated a total of 1,805,000. At this rate of growth, they are expected to number between 4,606,000 (low assumption) and 5,831,000 (high assumption) by 2000.

Since a considerable fraction of the nineteenth-century Coloured population was already living in towns, there was a parallel growth of the rural and urban sectors. Whereas in 1904 the ratios were approximately balanced, a sharp trend towards urbanization manifested itself in the 1946 census and has continued ever since. Of a total Coloured population of 1,509,258 in 1960, 68.5% were urban, residing chiefly in the larger cities and market towns of the Cape Province. Some have spread into the Transvaal and Natal urban centers, but their spiritual home remains the southwestern Cape. Here the Coloureds have found a firm niche in fruit canning, textile, clothing, furniture, and other skilled crafts and industries. Some 20% of the economically active population are engaged in manufacturing. Cape Coloured women have dominated the textile and clothing industries ever since they were established. At the same time, about 120,000 are still engaged as farm laborers in the vineyards, fruit orchards, and wheat fields or as fishermen operating from many of the Cape Peninsula's smaller harbors. Many of these are Cape Malays who, though classified as Coloured, retain all the elements of Islam.

Language as an Indicator. Lacking a cultural homeland, the Coloured have been forced to choose a language and a religion. Table 4 reveals a steady move towards Afrikaans as a home lan-

TABLE 4

Home Languages of the Coloured People

Year	*Afrikaans*	*English*	*Afrikaans and English*	*Others*
1936	690,151	58,646	7,888	12,976
1946	728,635	87,328	5,940	7,581
1951	982,998	108,133	8,559	3,326
1960	1,336,974	153,974	13,662	4,658

Sources: Statistical Year Book 1965, and *Union Statistics for Fifty Years 1910–1960.*

guage. In a cosmopolitan city such as Cape Town, most Coloureds are able to speak both official languages, but many prefer to be thought of as unilingually English, a reflection of local political attitudes, where Englishness is correlated with racial liberalism. The Cape Coloureds of Kimberley regard themselves as "English." A distinct dialect of Afrikaans is used by the less educated section, from which has emerged a distinguished vernacular poet with an international reputation.

Religion. Religious adherences also reflect the alternatives offered to the Coloureds (Table 5). The major religious faith of the country —the Calvinism of the Dutch Reformed Church—is also their dominant faith. Though less powerful numerically, the Anglican (Episcopal) Church holds sway over a large section of the various communities—a measure of continuing association not only with

English culture but also with early nineteenth-century Anglican missions who worked among the slaves and Hottentots. Several nonconformist religions have quite large followings. Within each community of Coloured there is also likely to be a subgroup of Muslim Malays, who build a mosque and spend their life savings on a pilgrimage to Mecca.

TABLE 5

Religions of the Coloured People

Religion	*1951*	*1960*
Dutch Reformed Church	291,087	442,944
Anglican	229,588	268,620
Roman Catholic	73,288	73,457
Congregational	112,295	137,358
Methodist	101,356	117,903
Muslim	63,216	93,256
Others	232,186	365,720
Total	870,830	1,133,538

Sources: Statistical Year Book 1965 and *Union Statistics for Fifty Years 1910–1960.*

Active missionary work on the part of the Dutch Reformed Church using the Afrikaans translation of the Bible is bringing in large numbers of converts, from which promising young men are ordained as ministers. There is not the same proliferation of Christian sects among the Coloured as there is among the Bantu, for example, who have managed to generate some 2,500 non-recognized schismatic churches in the Johannesburg area alone.

Demographic Characteristics. A glance at the vital statistics adequately explains the Coloured People's demographic ascendancy. Birth rates have remained consistently high despite a marked increase in urbanization during the past fifty years. Death rates have shown a marked decline, while infant mortality, though still shockingly high, has also fallen sharply in postwar years. These are the characteristics of a very "youthful" population, recognizable in any developing country (Table 6).

Understandably the Cape Coloured communities have a poor health record. Overcrowded urban slum conditions prevailing in Capetown and in other cities for several generations resulted not only in high infant mortality and a very high illegitimate birth rate but also in mass tuberculosis infection through all age ranges. Several helminthic and deficiency diseases were commonplace. That the situation is gradually improving is indicated by falling infant mortality and rising life expectation rates which have risen from 40 to 47 years at birth among males and from 41 to 49 years among females between 1935–37 and 1964–65. Alcoholism, particularly among rural vineyard workers, remains a health hazard.

TABLE 6

Demographic Statistics for the Coloured People

	1937	*1955*	*1960*	*1964*
Birth rates per thousand	47.1	45.4	46.6	46.6
Death rates per thousand	23.4	16.6	15.6	14.8
Natural increase per thousand		28.8	31.0	31.8
Infant mortality per thousand	165.9	134.5	128.6	115.7
Masculinity rate per thousand		101.8	101.3	101.4

Sources: Statistical Year Book 1965 and *Union Statistics for Fifty Years 1910–1960.*

Improved housing, welfare facilities, and a rising standard of living have been responsible for the improvement in towns and a number of peri-urban industrial areas. Many Coloured communities however are to be found in remote isolated parts of the northern Cape and South West Africa, unable to improve their lot. For many, the Orange River Project will therefore come as a great boon. Diamond mining companies on the Namaqualand coast have deliberately adopted a policy of employing the Coloured peoples of the Lower Orange River valley instead of migrant Bantu workers, in order to raise local living standards.

Demography and Politics. One of the most significant aspects of demographic vigor in the Coloured people is their role as political shuttlecocks during the last century, first in the Cape Colony and later in the Union. Because the white man "created" them, they have always pricked the conscience of the Cape politicians. While demographically speaking their influence was secondary, it was possible to grant franchise rights to the Coloured, not only during the period of responsible government in the Cape Colony, but later when the Union came into being.

Firmly entrenched in the Constitution of 1909, this right persisted until the preponderance of Coloured in the southwest Cape constituencies began seriously to interfere with the election of Nationalist candidates to the House of Assembly, since most Coloured voted with the opposition United Party. Their removal from the Common Roll in 1956, after a protracted constitutional struggle, was one of the first tasks which the Nationalist Government had set itself on coming into power in 1948. As recently as January 1967, the indeterminate role of the Coloureds in the future was the subject of a government Commission of Inquiry. Are they to be on the one hand a separate group, developing their undoubted talents as craftsmen, scholars, artists, and politicians (see page 162), or are they destined to merge with their white cousins, speaking the same languages and worshipping in the same churches? Despite many efforts, they have not found common political cause with Bantu and Indian groups. For many reasons, demography favors an alliance with white South Africa before all else, but to this question there can be no certain answer except emotional speculation.

THE ASIAN PEOPLE

With only very few exceptions, the term "Asiatic" applies to the East Indian or even more simply the Indian population. The remainder is chiefly Chinese; 5,000 Chinese speakers were recorded in the 1951 census. These are widely distributed throughout urban South Africa, as retail shopkeepers, laundrymen, importers, and in professional activities. Very little has been published on the modern Chinese community, but its demographic characteristics appear to resemble those of the whites more than any others. Of course, if the Chinese labor force, some 60,000 strong, used in the Witwatersrand gold mines in the first decade of this century had not been repatriated, there would have been an added ethnic complication.

Permanence of the Indian Settlement. There were an estimated 547,000 Indians living in South Africa in 1966, over 90% of whom were born in the country. They are descended either from indentured laborers of the untouchable caste, imported chiefly from Madras and Southern India, or from the traders and merchants who came via Mauritius or East Africa from Bombay. Despite powerful incentives offered by successive South African governments, few, except the aged, have ever returned to India. After completing their indentures, most remained in South Africa as gardeners and rice and tobacco farmers; they multiplied rapidly through natural increase supplemented by family immigration (on compassionate grounds) to more than half a million. Although they represent only 3% of the total population, the Indians have always been in the political limelight, mainly as a result of their limited distribution throughout South Africa.

Demographic Characteristics. The Indian population grew from 122,311 in 1904 to an estimated 547,000 by 1966, the greatest period of increase (30%) occurring between 1951 and 1960 (Table 7). Recent projections indicate that the total will be between 1,103,000 (557,000 males and 547,000 females) and 1,159,000 (585,000 males and 574,000 females) in the year 2000 assuming that immigration will play an insignificant part in the next few decades. Such an assumption may prove to be invalid, since refugee Indian communities from East Africa may seek shelter among their own kind in South Africa instead of returning to India.

There are several reasons for the sharp changes in rates of increase in the past. Although the Indian government insisted that for every 100 male laborers there should be 40 females accompanying them, when the Indian and Union government canceled the scheme in 1911, there was still a marked numerical imbalance between male and female Indians. Even though families and traders were allowed into the country, a corresponding adjustment in the masculinity ratio was slow in coming. This value changed from 998 per mille in 1955 to 1,004 in 1964. Secondly, the Spanish influenza pandemic struck heavily at the Indians, of whom some thousands died from it between 1918 and 1920.

TABLE 7

Population Data for the Asiatic Community
Average Annual

Year	*Population*	*Rate of Increase*	*No. of Females*	*Resident in Natal*	*Resident in Transvaal*
1904	122,311		39,712	100,918	10,948
1911	152,094	3.12	56,022	133,419	11,004
1921	163,594	0.73	67,433	141,060	14,503
1936	219,691	1.90	100,540	183,661	25,493
1946	285,260	2.65	136,184	232,317	37,758
1951	366,664	5.15	177,069	299,491	49,232
1960	477,125	2.87	235,488	394,854	63,787
1966	547,000 (estimate)		272,000		

Sources: Statistical Year Book 1965; Union Statistics for Fifty Years 1910–1960; Bureau of Census.

Indian demographic characteristics indicate a "youthful" community, though not as aggressively so as the Cape Coloured community. Crude birth rates are high—37.3 per thousand in 1938 and 33.3 in 1964—while crude death rates are very low—13.9 in 1938 and 7.4 per thousand in 1964. Infant mortality has fallen steadily from 94.7 per thousand live births in 1938 to 50.5 in 1964. Forty-five percent of the population in 1960 was less than 15 years old. A natural increase of 25.9 per thousand thus spells the continued expansion of a people detached from their motherland forever—a situation well known in Uganda, Kenya, Tanzania, Mauritius, Trinidad, Guyana, and Fiji. Life expectation for both males and females has also increased rapidly. For males, it rose from 50.70 years at birth to 55.77 and for females from 49.75 years to 54.75 between 1945–47 and 1950–52.

Contrary to general custom, South African Indians are monogamous, and illegitimate births are rare, indicating that the community is well adjusted to Western ways of life. The absence of miscegenation with other groups also makes for greater homogeneity.

Urbanization. The most prominent feature of Indian demography in the past fifty years has been the rapid rate of urbanization. The obvious gap in most South African communities towards the end of the nineteenth century was the trader, and when free from their indentures, many Indians chose the local trading store as a way of earning a living. They were rapidly followed by others from India who also seized their opportunities. The natural outcome was the creation of a trading community employed in import-export and retail activities. By 1960, more than 80% of the South African Indian community was urbanized, leaving the sugar cane fields to the Zulu, whose reluctance to engage in "women's work" had been the prime reason for introducing "coolie" labor.

More significant than demographic trends is the actual distribution of Indians in South Africa (Table 8). They are chiefly to be

TABLE 8

Urbanization of South African Indians
(in thousands)

Year	*Total*	*Urban*	*% Urban*	*Number Urban who reside in Natal*
1904	122	44	36.5	24
1911	152	80	52.8	63
1921	164	99	60.4	77
1936	220	153	69.5	120
1946	285	208	72.8	158
1951	367	285	77.6	221
1960	477	397	83.2	318

Sources: Statistical Year Book 1965 and *Union Statistics for Fifty Years 1910–1960.*

found in Natal, their original subtropical destination, and to a lesser degree in the Transvaal. By 1910 they had outnumbered the whites of Natal, and today not only are there more Indian school children than white in the province, but they claim a lion's share of the educational budget. Politically, however, they have regressed from a nineteenth century qualified franchise to disenfranchisement in the twentieth, mainly as a consequence of their growing numbers and economic strength in Natal. Not only in the towns but also in the countryside they fulfilled their traditional commercial role of moneylender to black and white alike on crops not yet harvested, bartering goods for corn which they resold, with interest, to the original owners in the hungry season, thus prospering against all odds. Thus came into being yet another racial stereotype—the Indian trader "living on the smell of an oilrag," deeply resented by all who were in his debt and suffering on more than one occasion from violent reactions to this "exploitation."

Despite a number of restrictions placed upon them, Indians have generally prospered in all the towns of Natal and Transvaal. They are deeply involved not only as industrial workmen, but as large-scale owners of textile, clothing, and other factories. Though many have accumulated considerable wealth, using it not only to build handsome clubs and houses but also schools, temples, cinemas, and commercial buildings, half of the Indian community lives near or below the breadline.

The Indian as a South African. In other parts of the country, it has proved more difficult for Indians to become stabilized. The Orange Free State introduced severe restrictions on permanent Asiatic immigration in 1890 so that in 1967 there are virtually no Indians living and owning property within its boundaries. After several attempts, the Transvaal Republic acquired powers to prevent Asiatics from acquiring property, mining licenses, and citizenship as well as to restrict them to certain sections of any town. Indian traders were allowed to circumvent these restrictions on the grounds that they provided a service which the pastoral Boer would not deign to touch. They are in their thousands firmly settled as scattered communities in Johannesburg and other towns and are therefore severely affected by the Group Areas Act. The Cape Colony made feeble attempts to apply a number of immigration restrictions, but were able only to prevent Indians from entering the Bantu reserves of Kaffraria, Transkei, and Pondoland. Small numbers of Indians are found today in most of the large towns of the Cape Province.

At the instigation of Mahatma Gandhi, a practicing lawyer in South Africa, the government of India took up the cudgels on behalf of its expatriate Indian population from 1894 onwards, in the hope that repatriation might eliminate this thorny problem; and the Union Government continued until 1946 to regard Indians as aliens. Succeeding generations born in South Africa have gradually reduced such assumptions to absurdity, and though not granted universal franchise, the South African Indians are now considered to be a permanent part of the Republic.

Abandoning Asian loyalties, however, has not caused the Indian to relinquish his languages, religion, or faiths completely. Education in a large city like Durban is therefore complicated by the use of several Indian tongues in addition to English and Afrikaans (Table 9). Most Indians in Durban understand, speak, and read English,

TABLE 9

Asiatic Languages in South Africa—1951

Language	*Number Speaking It as Home Language*
Tamil	120,181
Hindi	89,145
Gujerati	39,495
Telegu	30,210
Urdu	25,456
Other Indian	26,090
Chinese	4,738
Other	1,037
Unspecified	245

Source: Union Statistics for Fifty Years 1910–1960.

while a large percentage in the Cape and the Transvaal can also speak Afrikaans. Continuous efforts are being made to maintain an Indian home language, if not in public schools, then in private institutions. Books, vernacular newspapers and movies in each language are imported. Debased forms of Tamil and Hindi are most commonly used in Natal, while in the Transvaal Gujerati is predominant, but all are in rapid decline among the young people.

A further complication on the cultural landscape is the presence of several non-Christian religions among the Indian population (Table 10). Though these do not produce communal riots, they do serve to bring about separate groupings within a given community and add another administrative difficulty to the educational system. Besides 30,000 Christian Indians (mostly Catholic) nearly 60,000 Muslims and 283,000 Hindus were living in Natal in 1960.

TABLE 10

Religions of Asiatics in South Africa—1960

Name	*Number of Adherents*
Islam	98,490
Hindu	310,839
Other unspecified	33,517
Christians	34,259
Total	477,125

Source: Statistical Year Book 1965.

Rising Standards of Living. The socioeconomic status of women and girls within South African Indian society has until recently followed traditional conservative lines. Child marriages are still negotiated, and unlimited families are regarded as insurance policies against old age. Indian merchants prefer to employ Coloured or white typists rather than their own girls, while few Indian women (less than 5%) have found their way into any industry or profession except teaching. That change is coming can be confirmed in the playgrounds of the many Durban schools where Indian girls can be seen engaged in Swedish drill, basketball, or softball, garbed in shorts and shirt.

Though seriously deficient in protein foods, affected by helminthic and amebic infections, tuberculosis, and typhoid, the Indian population has rapidly improved in health through improved housing, subsidized foods, and widespread medical and welfare facilities, including family-planning clinics. It has, with a few individual exceptions, readily accepted separate development (pages 162–163), especially in cities as large as Durban, where socioeconomic stratification has replaced caste systems. Since most indentured immigrants were "untouchables," it is not surprising that this step came about voluntarily without any need for anticaste legislation.

MIGRATION PATTERNS

Human mobility is not a marked feature of the white people of South Africa despite a long history of mass migrations and restless wanderings in the nineteenth century. Regional loyalties, language differences, and cultural schism have prevented the kind of change which characterizes so much of North American life.

Rural "poor whites" are a major exception, long isolated by historical circumstances. They have surged into the metropolitan centers, but once there tend to settle down. Only those in the Civil Service, the nationally managed railroads and harbors services, or police and armed forces would expect to face regular transfers from one place to another. In Angola, Patagonia, and Brazil there are to be found relict farming communities descended from Boer rebels who preferred exile to the British flag after the Anglo-Boer War (1899–1902). Since 1950, numbers of academicians, politicians, and others have emigrated or fled from government policies.

The Bantu, restricted by law from free movement into the cities, have nonetheless slowly migrated as far west as Cape Town, competing with Coloureds for unskilled jobs, and as has been shown (pages 56–57), now occupy an indispensable sector of every city and industry in the country. Though tied to his home reserve, the migrant laborer often chooses to take a succession of jobs in new places and widen his acquaintance with the country. Many members of the Bantu intelligentsia, as well as a number of politicians, have also emigrated to the United Kingdom, the United States, or to other African countries in order to avoid the consequences of a number of the country's racial laws. Some have developed into professional refugees in certain countries.

Among the Cape Coloured and Indian communities, local loyalties generally override the urge to move permanently away from the birthplace. Many Cape Coloureds, in search of racial equality and greater opportunity, have emigrated to multiracial or apparently race-tolerant areas such as the West Indies, the United Kingdom, and Canada. They are more commonly the darker-skinned members of a family, some of whom have managed to "pass for white." The latter, therefore, will even subsidize such emigrations in order to avoid investigation by a Race Classification Board.

In common with other developing, industrializing countries, South Africa has received many immigrants, black and white, during the past century. About one million foreign Africans are estimated to be in the country at any one time as contract laborers, or as legal or illegal migrants from as far afield as East Africa. Indians have also been smuggled ashore or across the long Mozambique frontier.

White immigrants have come in a slight but steady stream to take their place mainly in mining, industry, and commerce. Between 1945 and 1948 the government made halfhearted attempts to divert emigrants going to Canada, the United States, and Australia. The National Party, fearing the effects on Afrikaans culture and religion of large-scale immigration of Roman Catholics, non-Nordic Europeans and English speakers, withdrew its support from the program. Since 1962, government policy has once more been directed towards attracting as many skilled white people as possible to South Africa, by offering subsidized transport and other financial benefits.

Some influential discontent has been expressed among conservative right-wing Afrikaners about the large numbers of Greeks and Portuguese who are entering the country under these schemes. The main fear is that the numerical preponderance of the Afrikaans-speaking is likely to disappear within thirty years at the present rate of immigration, since most of the newcomers will augment the English-speaking communities. Whether such xenophobic chauvinism can survive all the demographic pressures bearing on South Africa is not known, but it cannot altogether be discounted. Many members of the ruling party are willing to support a move which would restrict "Paradise" only to the pure in heart—the Netherlander, the German, and the Flemish Belgian, all of whom would be expected to gravitate towards Afrikanerdom.

Immigration and Christian liberalism in the Dutch Reformed Church are, in fact, two topics which threaten the monolithic unity of the Afrikaans community. It is possible to distinguish separate groups which hold divergent views. The first belong to the *verligtes* (enlightened, outward looking, open-society types); the second are said to be *verkramptes* (conservative, inward looking, closed-society types). That they exist is evidence of a growing maturity of outlook in at least one section of the Afrikaans community.

4 Roots of the South African Economy

AMONG THE world's nations, only Japan outranks South Africa in economic growth. Despite a formidable list of physical difficulties, the country has become the economic giant of the African continent. It ranks twelfth among the world's trading nations and shows every sign of remaining there. With 6% of Africa's area and only 5% of its population, South Africa produces more than 75% of the steel produced and 45% of the entire continent's industrial products. What accounts, we may ask, for this astonishing growth from an agglomeration of ill-assorted agrarian territories into a highly organized industrial country?

ECONOMIC GROWTH

Most modern economic theorists generally look to the agricultural sector in any developing or emergent country to supply the capital for subsequent growth. It has already been shown that agriculture in South Africa suffers many serious drawbacks and therefore cannot have been responsible for this metamorphosis, except in a negative way. It was mineral wealth and its exploitation which offered the primary basis for industrial growth. That South Africa was able to make the transition from mining to manufacture within a generation, and at the same time to drag its farming sector from the eighteenth into the twentieth century, must still be regarded as a modern miracle.

The Role of Minerals. There was, of course, a fortunate overlap of events and mining discoveries which favored the gradual development of all the country's vast resources without exhausting the reserves of one mineral before the next came to light. Also, profits from one mineral provided the capital for exploiting the next and thus laid the foundations for one of the world's most important mining empires.

The accidental discovery of diamonds in Griqualand West in 1867 was but the first step in a chain of events which finally scotched the Voortrekkers' dream of a rural utopia on the highveld and instead set in motion an industrial revolution. Early finds in the gravels and dry channels of the Orange River brought more than 50,000 pioneers from all parts of the world to the area between 1867 and 1870. Most of them, however, moved to individual claims on the yellow weathered rocks of several old volcanic throats or pipes. Although many personal fortunes were made (and lost) during the following 20 years, it was personalities like Cecil Rhodes and his contemporaries which impressed themselves on the area and forced the consolidation of all the claims into a single holding. New mining techniques made it possible to extract diamonds from the "blue ground," the unweathered *kimberlite* which had been considered sterile, and to bring Cecil Rhodes the fortune he required to embark on a political career (pages 99–100). His partners' fortunes went to the development of the gold mines of the Witwatersrand, dating from 1886 onward, which today yield 75% of the free world's gold.

The Modern Economy. The need for fuel led in turn to coal mining in northern Natal and the Transvaal and more notably to the laying of a railroad to bring coal to the Witwatersrand. A hungry appetite for commercial explosives for rock blasting created a vast chemical complex. Twentieth-century fears for gold as an international means of exchange and two world wars were the means of effecting industrial revolution by diversification, manufacturing based on local raw materials, and exports. The capital needed to carry out this program was derived from taxation of gold production, from surplus funds of the gold and diamond mining companies, and later, from overseas investment. This transition from a rural frontier community to a modern industrial society was made in little more than eighty years, but in some respects the economy still rests upon the continued exploitation and sale of precious and base minerals.

AGRICULTURE

The Victualing Station. The successful attempt of the Dutch East India Company to create a small gardening colony around their fort in Table Bay emphasizes the favorable terrain and climate of the southwestern Cape. Huguenot refugees some twenty years later (in 1688) laid the foundations of what was to be a highly successful vine and fruit cultivation. The sandy soils of the Zandveld to the north of Table Bay yielded wheat until their virgin fertility declined to an unproductive zero and forced the first local farmers to look to livestock rearing for a living. For nearly a hundred years thereafter the *veeboer* (nomadic stockfarmer) sidled eastward in search of pastures for his cattle and drove them to Cape Town so that the Company could have beef to sell to passing ships.

In the deep valleys of Paarl, Stellenbosch, and Worcester, men pressed grapes into a wine considered good enough to be drunk by Metternich and his confrères at the Congress of Vienna in 1815. Wheat and vine continued to grow side by side in these valleys, and slaves grew vegetables for Cape Town and its ships.

These were the pioneer techniques of the past. To a large extent they survived into this century. Markets may have changed, but little else. Maize, a simple cereal crop suited to the soils of the highveld, was added to the *veeboer*'s cattle ranch and became the standard agricultural crop for subsistence and sale.

Sheep Ranching. A major exception to this general pattern was sheep farming. The scrawny fat-tailed sheep of the Hottentots were well known to local Dutch farmers as a meat source. The first wooled sheep imported from Holland in 1657 failed to meet the high standards of European wool markets, and despite continual efforts by the Company, wool exports ceased from the Cape in 1718. The introduction of the Spanish merino breed 70 years later immediately restored wool as a cash crop among the farmers of the eastern Cape. A small mill set up by a blanket maker from Somerset, England, survived for several years in the small Border town of Bathurst. By 1856, there were more than one million wooled merino sheep in South Africa, distributed throughout the northern Cape, Orange Free State and Transvaal by the Voortrekkers. Wool is today second only to gold in exports, being the pastoral product of a largely pastoral country (Table 11). Some 40 million sheep,

TABLE 11

Distribution of Wool Exports 1964–1965

Destination	*Grease Bales*	*Scoured Bales*
United Kingdom	149,489	19,119
France	137,826	6,054
U.S.A.	128,973	14,560
Japan	116,350	2,367
Germany	108,562	6,054
Italy	89,232	5,996

Note: A bale weighs between 280 and 300 lb.
Source: Standard Bank Review.

90% of which are kept for the wool clip, are found on the Karroo and highveld, where they can survive climatic rigors and moderate quality grazing. As many as one million lambs (less than one year old) die annually as a result of drought and lack of pasture. One of the aims of the Orange River Project is the elimination of such waste by supplementary feeding (see page 131). Transhumance of flocks is still practiced from the Orange Free State to the Drakensberg slopes, where early burning provides a flush of green grass in the winter months—much to the detriment of the veld and therefore strongly discouraged. Six countries took 70% of the total clip in the 1964–65, the remaining 30% being absorbed by local weaving and cloth industries.

Most of South Africa's wool production is in the hands of about 30,000 white farmers in the Cape (66%), Orange Free State (23%), and the Transvaal (8%). They send their clip to Port Elizabeth, East London, Durban, and Cape Town for sale by public auction, between September and May. A levy is charged on all wool sold, in order to establish a stabilization fund for price support and promotion facilities in the face of increasing competition from synthetic fibres.

Karakul Production. Though less significant numerically, the Karakul sheep, a breed imported from Turkestan in 1907, thrives in the driest areas of the northwest Cape and South-West Africa. The pelts of newborn lambs are made into expensive fashion "fur" coats while the mature wools are used in carpet manufacture. They offer a living in areas which would normally be agriculturally unusable. Some 1.4 million Karakul sheep are found in the Republic and another 3 million in South-West Africa. Most of the luxury coat assembly is now carried out in Windhoek.

A small number of Angora goats, yielding high-quality mohair, are also found in the Eastern Cape, but have been replaced in part by the more profitable merino, mainly as a result of the introduction of jackal fencing. Other goat breeds are discouraged in view of the considerable damage they can inflict on soils and vegetation.

Bantu Sheep Farming. Sheep farming is a sporadic farming activity among the Bantu peoples. A number of farmers in the Transkei and Ciskei run large flocks for wool, and the entire production of Lesotho (Basutoland) is brought into the Republic for disposal. Among cattle-keeping communities, sheep and goats are merely kept for their meat and become significant only in areas where the veld has degenerated under grazing pressures. They are occasionally milked during periods of food shortage, but no attempt is made to convert goat's milk to cheese.

Cattle. Cattle have for different reasons played a vital role in the lives of Bantu and White nations alike. To the Bantu they represented wealth, prestige, and religion (pages 31–32); to the White pastoralist they represented an object for trade, to be sold on the hoof in Cape Town after a long drive west from the interior or broken down into hides, lard, and the traditional sun-dried meat, *biltong*.

To draw his wagon trains, the white pastoralist (*veeboer* or *trekboer*) used indigenous, humped red animals identifiable as a separate breed known as the Afrikander. Able to withstand great heat and rough pastures the breed spread as far as the tsetse fly would allow it to go. Its value as a trek ox, together with its glamorized role in the folk myth of the Voortrekkers, delayed for many years the development of a beef industry based on more suitable breeds. Change came suddenly with the importation and acclimatizing of European beef and dairy breeds after rinderpest had decimated the local stock in 1897.

Crossbreeding with local Afrikander and Bantu varieties have produced animals which thrive in the savanna areas of the Transvaal bushveld and lowveld under extensive Texas-like ranching conditions. Elsewhere, as in the southern Cape, the Natal midlands, and the eastern Transvaal, European breeds have, with supplementary feeding, proved to be successful high-quality beef producers. Occasionally a surplus has been available for export, but until larger areas are available for cultivating alfalfa (lucerne) under irrigation, this will remain slight. Maize and sorghum are not yet fully utilized to condition beef cattle for the market. Botswana, Swaziland, and South-West Africa export beef cattle to the Republic.

Dairy Production. The dairy cattle industry has grown with urban and industrial expansion, until recently concentrated for the most part (through a legal accident) within the city limits of the eight metropolitan areas. The Friesan, Ayrshire, Brown Swiss, Shorthorn, Jersey, and Guernsey breeds have had little difficulty in adapting themselves to the cooler, moister regions below the Escarpment, where distance from markets has resulted in factories producing cheese, butter, and powdered or condensed milk. In good years it has been possible to export significant quantities of butter and powdered milk, not only to Europe but also to the other African and Asian countries, but owing to local population increase and rising standards of living, it is doubtful whether export will be possible in the future.

Cattle Among the Bantu. Of South Africa's 13 million head of cattle, at least 5,000,000 are Bantu-owned in reservations or on white farmlands. Traditional attitudes have until recently prevented these animals from entering the cattle trade. Poor in quality, inbred, and often disease-prone, such animals would not qualify for a reasonable sale price, but in order to eliminate the vast surplus on Bantu grazing lands, many efforts have been directed towards establishing centers for stock sales and breeding studs for raising the quality of the herds. Many of these schemes have been conspicuously successful among the tribes with progressive chiefs who have increased dairy as well as beef production without any difficulty. A deboning factory in the Transkei is rapidly increasing its output (see page 159) as more and more animals are sold at district auction sales, effectively protected from speculative buyers. It is not unlikely that with such instructive examples in mind, Bantu attitudes towards cattle will veer rapidly away from the traditional towards the economic.

Other Livestock. From its earliest days in the Cape, the Dutch East India Company imported Arab horses for local use. From them developed a hardy ranging animal which, when cross-bred with English thoroughbreds after the British seizure of the Cape in 1795, not only provided the pastoral farmers (*veeboere*) with excellent mounts, but also in due course persuaded the Sotho and Pondo to adopt the horse. An extensive horse trade developed with India in the supply of cavalry remounts, and later with British forces in South Africa itself during the Anglo-Boer wars. Apart from the Sotho and the Pondo, most Bantu tribes failed to take advantage of the mobility offered by the horse. A Zulu army mounted in battle offers a terrifying prospect, and yet it did not happen. Donkeys are found over most of South Africa and in some places are a pest. They are used as draught and pack animals along with mules.

Poultry and pig farming have rapidly developed, particularly in Natal and the Transvaal near urban areas. Considerable quantities of eggs are normally available for export from highly efficient farming units, but changing consumer habits in the Bantu urban communities are gradually reducing this kind of surplus, for until recently eggs were taboo to the womenfolk as an item in their diet.

No account of South Africa would be complete without some reference to the ostrich farming of the eastern Cape, where prosperity fluctuates according to the fashions.

Pioneer Farming of Grains. If cattle and sheep dominated a large sector of the South African economy, then the traditional monoculture of maize played an equally important part in preventing arable farming from modernizing its production techniques. Maize was introduced via West African slave ships to the southwest Cape but met with little success. As the frontier extended into the interior, more favorable climatic conditions made it an important subsistence crop among white pastoralists. It quickly displaced sorghum (Kaffir corn) as the chief cereal crop grown by the Bantu womenfolk.

With livestock and maize the white farmer considered himself self-sufficient and established a tradition of subsistence agriculture which proved difficult to break down. Lands repeatedly planted to maize, without fertilizers or improved seeds, yielded to soil erosion, baring large areas in the early twentieth century. Yet within forty years it has been possible by various means to correct all these errors and in most years to reap from the highveld and Natal enough maize to feed the republic and provide a surplus for export to a number of countries.

In the Bantu reservations, maize has proved a fickle friend. Planted without regard to contours on steep hillsides, without improved seed, manures, or mineral fertilizers, it has steadily declined in yield over the years. All too frequently, serious droughts deprive a large number of communities of any crop at all. For such dilemmas, there can be only one solution: diversification and modernization, both of which have come very slowly among peoples who continue to believe firmly in magic and ritual as part of the cropping timetable.

Confined for many years within the winter rainfall area of the Cape, wheat has migrated northeastward to the eastern Orange Free State, the Lesotho lowlands, the Transvaal bushveld and the Vaal-Hartz irrigation areas. Despite continued expansion of the total crop yield, South Africa continues to be a net importer, mainly because wheat bread is being eaten by Bantu families now able to afford it. Additional areas suited to wheat are limited, however, and only the additional irrigated lands of the Orange River Project will allow any significant increase in yields, which will certainly not bring self-sufficiency. Canada, Australia, and the United States will continue to supply the rest.

Rice has long been a "vegetable" food not only in the Indian diet, but throughout the country. During World War II, broken white maize was used as a substitute for unobtainable rice, highlighting the need for extensive local cultivation. Despite the considerable efforts in Swaziland and in the Pongola Valley of northern Natal, it appears that only 10% of the country's requirements can be met locally.

Fruit Farming. Fruit farming goes back to the earliest settlements of the Cape when vines, deciduous fruits, and citrus were cultivated by the Huguenots. The deep valleys and protected slopes of the southwest folded mountains have remained the home of viticulture and extensive wine-brandy manufacture. There are today at least 5,000 growers whose wines find a ready market in thirty countries.

Deciduous fruit cultivation is found chiefly within a radius of 100 miles from Cape Town in the neighborhood of Port Elizabeth. Together with citrus, grown in the Transvaal, the lowveld, and the eastern and western Cape, and a wide range of tropical fruits from coastal Natal and the lowveld, it provides a large part of the country's agricultural exports to Europe and North America. Coming from the southern hemisphere in refrigerated ships, they are able to meet the off-season demands of the northern countries. Canned fruits and vegetables, processed according to the highest standards, are also sold abroad as well as locally. There appears to be no limit to this market, and under expert technical management exports are expected to double within the next ten years. Progressive Bantu farmers are being drawn into fruit production in small numbers.

Sugar. Subtropical varieties of sugar cane imported from Mauritius to Natal in the mid-nineteenth century have spread into the irrigated lands of Swaziland, Transvaal lowveld, and the Pongola Valley.

Bantu growers in coastal Zululand have adopted sugar as a cash crop. The industry, a closely integrated arrangement of mills and refineries, satisfies all local requirements with a surplus for export, particularly to Japan and Great Britain, and under the quota system, to the U.S.A. For many years, this surplus was converted to a high-octane automobile spirit, but much of it is now going into molasses, the manufacture of gin, rum, and other alcoholic liquors.

Other Cash Crops. Cotton growing, established in 1909, had a checkered history despite its obvious promise. Only after World War II, when textile mills were set up, did production begin to increase. High-quality long-staple varieties are grown along the Middle Orange River Valley, and wherever irrigation is possible, cotton is a primary cash crop on the eastern side of the Escarpment. Bantu growers have gradually adopted the crop in the Pongola area and seem likely to take it up in the irrigable lands of the Transkei (see page 159). Cottonseed oil has become a valuable byproduct, and together with a rapidly expanding groundnut and sunflower-seed industry, provides much of the country's vegetable oils.

Virginia-type tobacco thrives in the central and northern Transvaal, northern Free State, and eastern Cape, while the Turkish type is grown in the southwest Cape. Large quantities of cured leaf tobacco are exported to Europe and returned as cigarettes, but locally manufactured cigarettes appear to be able to compete with those imported from the U.S.A. and Great Britain, and are exported to many countries.

With a view to self-sufficiency, South Africa has begun to cultivate a number of hitherto imported crops. Tea, once grown in Natal, has again been planted in the Barberton district and Tzaneen areas of the Eastern Transvaal, the Natal midlands, and Zululand. The first crop will be reaped in 1968 and by 1972 is expected to yield 6 million pounds. Experiments at Lambasi in the Transkei have led to the establishment of 1,260 acres of tea bushes, to be cultivated by local Bantu farmers. Import substitution is also to be sought for coffee, pyrethrum, and sisal. Large acres of New Zealand flax (*phormium tenax*) are already yielding a jute substitute in the Transkei, although the use of brown paper "string" woven into "cloth" has effectively displaced jute as a baling material for cotton and wool, resulting in decreasing contamination of the latter.

Horticulture. Intensive horticulture has shown remarkable progress in the past two decades. Portuguese gardeners, who successfully monopolized the large Johannesburg market, are meeting strong competition from the Transvaal lowveld, which, with its favorable climatic conditions, is likely to be the future vegetable garden of much of the highveld. Indian gardeners have also had to face this competition, particularly as industrial progress in greater Durban steadily eliminates their suburban small holdings. Cape Town, dominated by Cape Coloured and Malay smallholders, may in the distant future receive vegetables from certain irrigation areas of the Lower Orange, when the Orange River Project has been completed (see page 131). Experimental air-freight loads, 30 tons at a time, of green vegetables are now being flown to European markets.

The Future of Agriculture. In reviewing the remarkable advances made by South African agriculture against the odds of drought, disease, floods, and world depression, it would be difficult to isolate a single reason for the change. There is abundant evidence of rising productivity resulting from improved varieties, greater use of mineral fertilizers, conservation practices, irrigation, rural electrification, and most of all, mechanization (Table 12). Locally manufactured trac-

TABLE 12

Tractors in White Farming Areas

Year	*Number*
1937	6,019
1945	20,292
1960	121,000
1962	127,000

Source: Statistical Year Book 1965.

tors have released oxen and Bantu laborers from an age-old bondage. Droughts, locusts and recession have shaken out the surplus rural communities from their marginal strongholds and forced them to abandon farming lands which were becoming increasingly fragmented as a result of the Roman-Dutch laws of inheritance, and creating the so-called poor white communities.

In many instances, overcapitalization and overgenerous Land Bank loans after World War II also contributed to the marginal farming downfall. Most important of all to agricultural development has been the successful use of marketing and control boards which have been able to offer the farmer guaranteed minimum prices in a reasonably well-protected market, as well as rational collection and distribution procedures, while at the same time demanding improved quality from the producer.

There has also been a significant growth of agricultural cooperative organizations (over 300 in 1967) which dispose of all the country's wine, tobacco, and alfalfa crops, most of the grains, 80% of the citrus, and 60% of the wool clip. Farmers in turn purchase much of their equipment, fertilizers, and seed from their cooperatives. In view of the very great expenditure on water storage, hydroelectric power, and irrigation projected throughout the country over the next thirty years, it is clear that, if there are enough South African farmers to take advantage of the schemes, their yields and productivity can only rise.

Whether the same immediate optimism can be expressed for Bantu agriculture is not yet certain. Similar losses of "farmers" from the land have taken place. Women have replaced men at the plough and make good farmers. Demonstrations, technical advice, education, cooperatives, and mechanization are all bringing changes to those who remain on the land in Bantu reservations. The Transkei is an example of how quickly and dramatically improvement can come to lands which were considered to be doomed only a decade ago. It is barely possible that Zululand will be able to save its soil in the same way, but time is not on its side. Much will depend on the fate of the Bantu Homelands Policy of the present government. Removing a greater part of the rural farming population from the land and placing it in the nonagricultural sector is an essential part of the policy (pages 159–160). Can this be done before the remaining agricultural lands collapse?

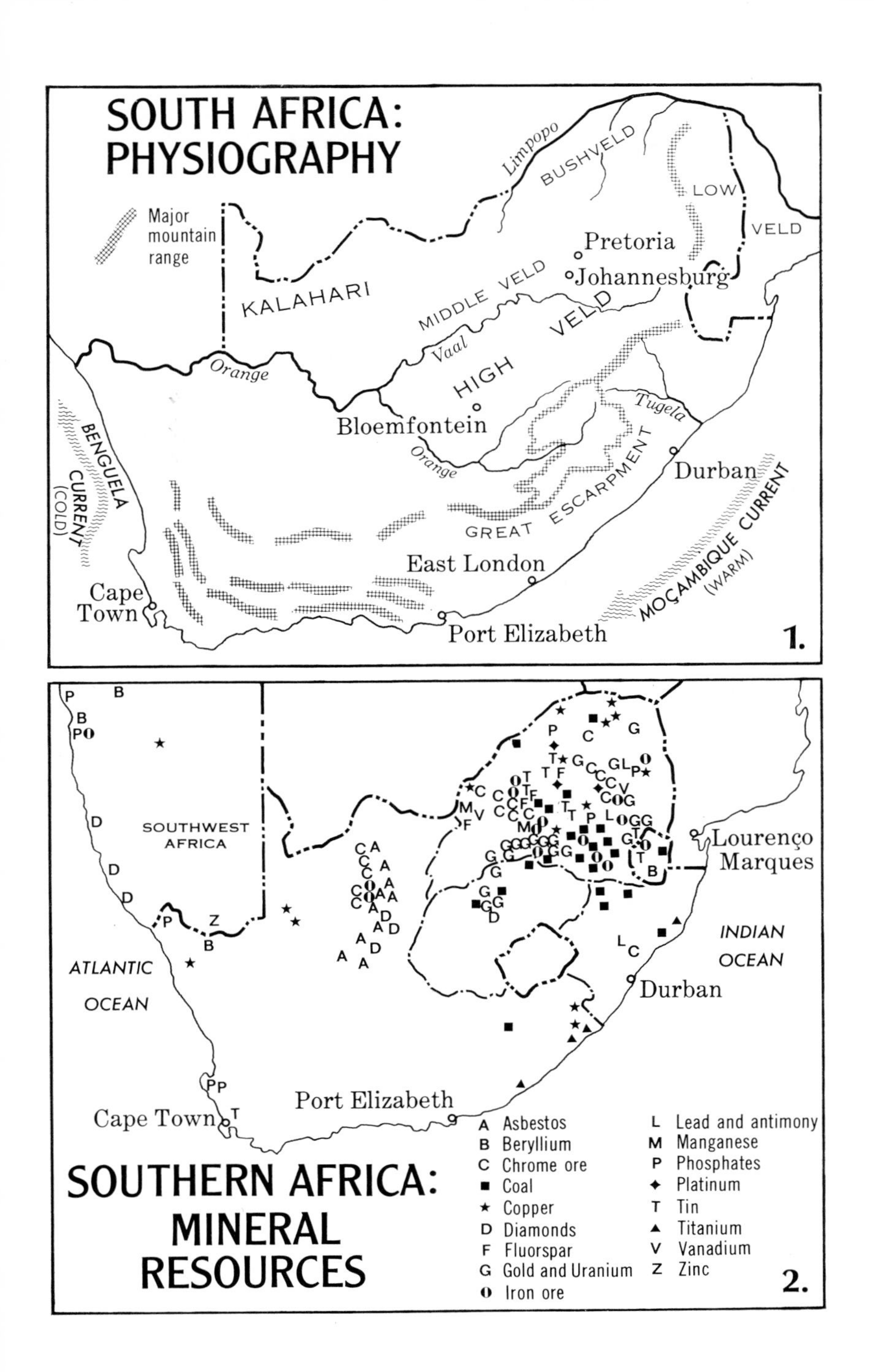
SOUTH AFRICA: PHYSIOGRAPHY
Major mountain range
Limpopo
BUSHVELD
LOW
VELD
Pretoria
Johannesburg
KALAHARI
MIDDLE VELD
HIGH VELD
Vaal
Orange
Tugela
Bloemfontein
BENGUELA CURRENT (COLD)
Durban
GREAT ESCARPMENT
MOÇAMBIQUE CURRENT (WARM)
East London
Cape Town
Port Elizabeth
1.
SOUTHWEST AFRICA
Lourenço Marques
INDIAN OCEAN
ATLANTIC OCEAN
Durban
Port Elizabeth
Cape Town
SOUTHERN AFRICA: MINERAL RESOURCES
A Asbestos
B Beryllium
C Chrome ore
■ Coal
★ Copper
D Diamonds
F Fluorspar
G Gold and Uranium
O Iron ore
L Lead and antimony
M Manganese
P Phosphates
✦ Platinum
T Tin
▲ Titanium
V Vanadium
Z Zinc
2.

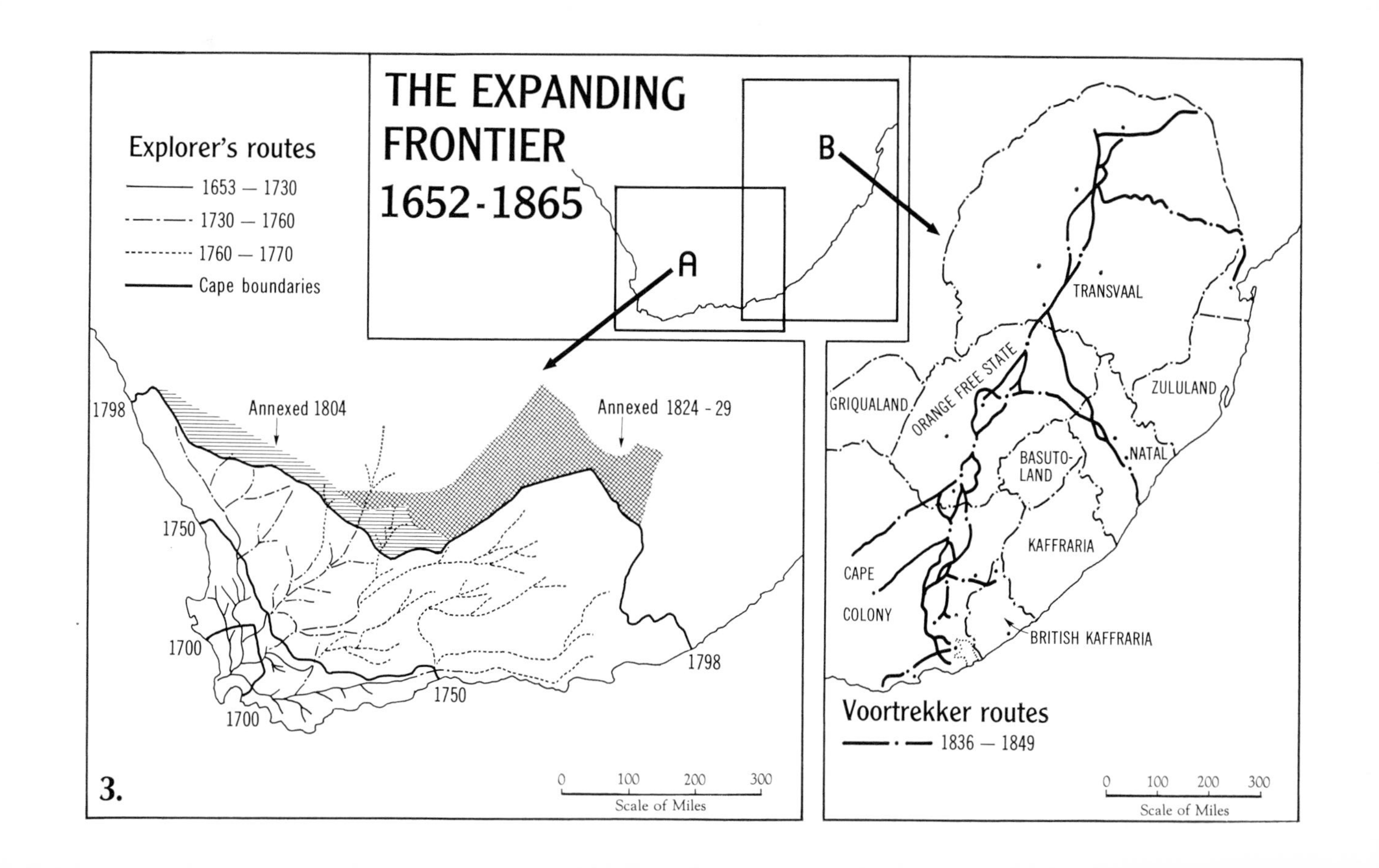
THE EXPANDING FRONTIER 1652-1865
Explorer's routes
1653 — 1730
1730 — 1760
1760 — 1770
Cape boundaries
A
B
1798
Annexed 1804
Annexed 1824 - 29
1750
1700
1700
1750
1798
3.
0
100
200
300
Scale of Miles
TRANSVAAL
GRIQUALAND
ORANGE FREE STATE
ZULULAND
NATAL
BASUTO-
LAND
KAFFRARIA
CAPE
COLONY
BRITISH KAFFRARIA
Voortrekker routes
1836 — 1849
0
100
200
300
Scale of Miles

POPULATION PROJECTIONS

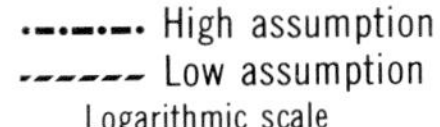

Logarithmic scale

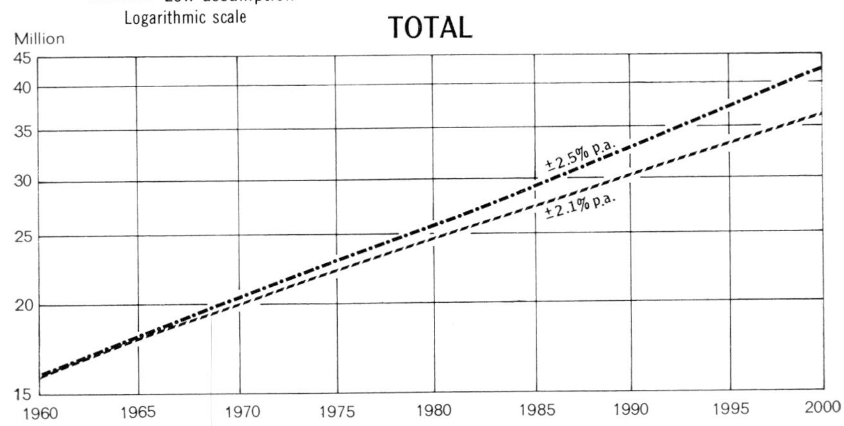

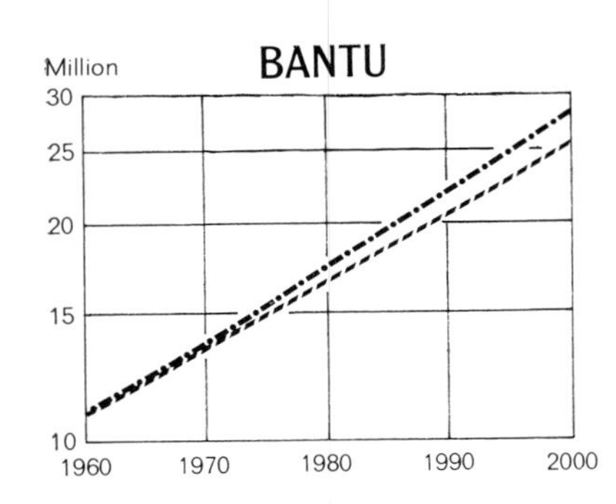

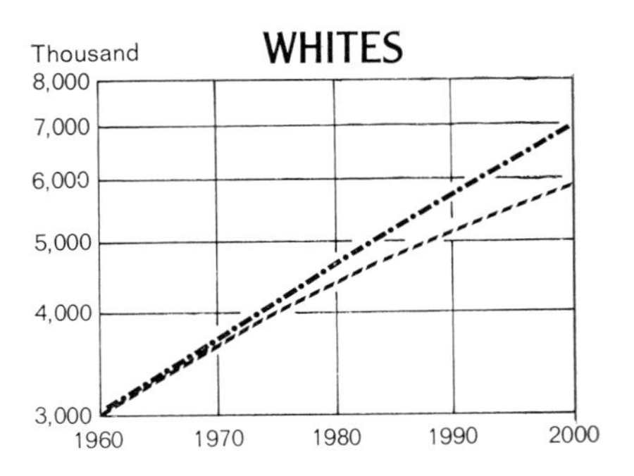

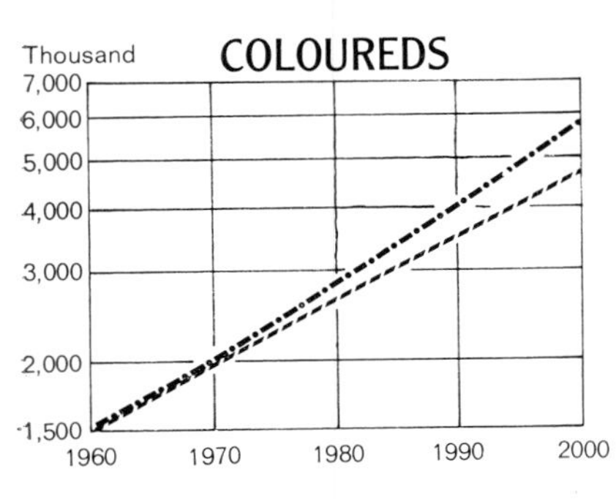

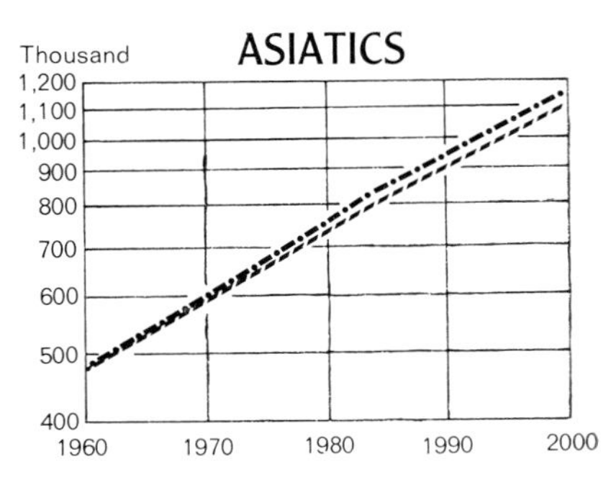

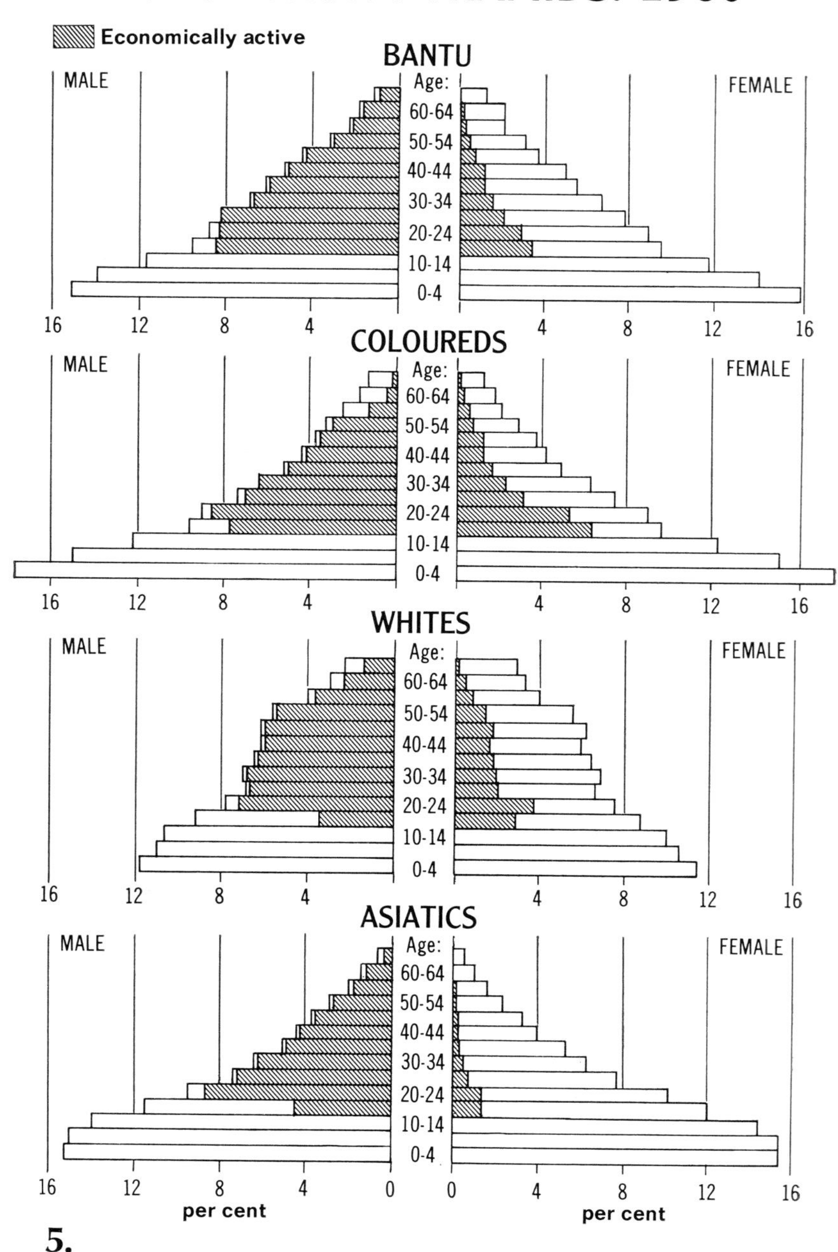
POPULATION PYRAMIDS: 1960
Economically active
BANTU
MALE
FEMALE
Age:
60-64
50-54
40-44
30-34
20-24
10-14
0-4
16
12
8
4
COLOUREDS
WHITES
ASIATICS
0
per cent
per cent

5.

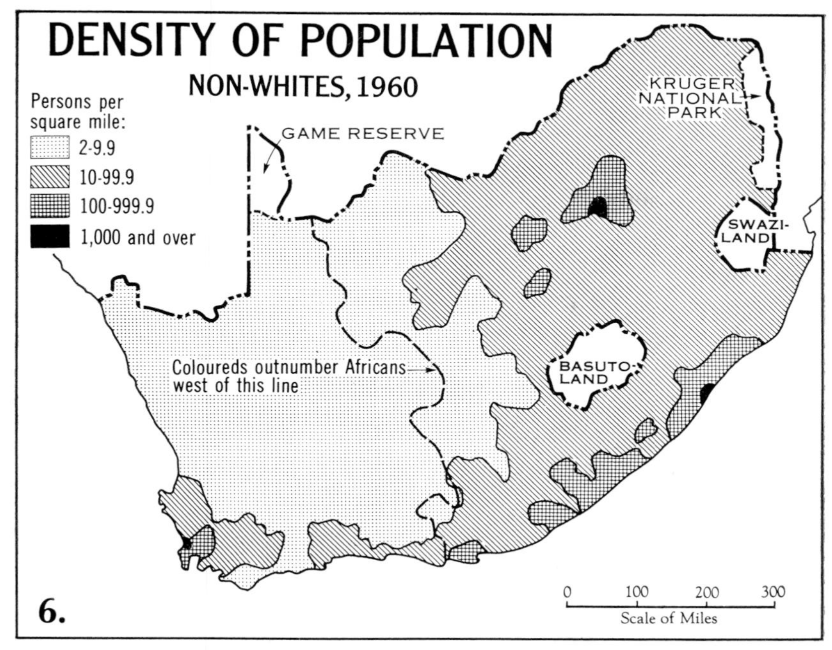
DENSITY OF POPULATION
NON-WHITES, 1960
Persons per square mile:
2-9.9
10-99.9
100-999.9
1,000 and over
GAME RESERVE
KRUGER NATIONAL PARK
SWAZI-LAND
BASUTO-LAND
Coloureds outnumber Africans west of this line
0 100 200 300
Scale of Miles
6.

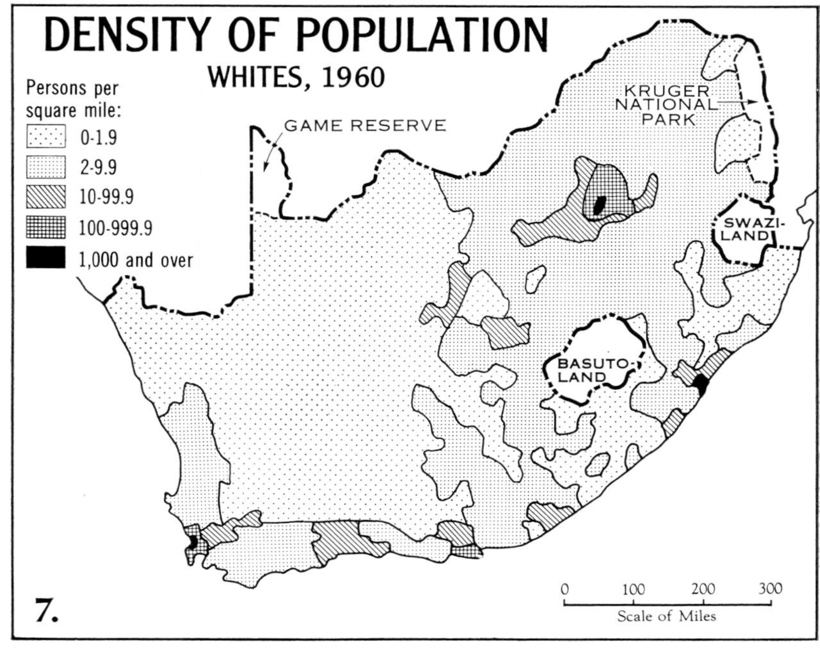
DENSITY OF POPULATION
WHITES, 1960
Persons per square mile:
0-1.9
2-9.9
10-99.9
100-999.9
1,000 and over
GAME RESERVE
KRUGER NATIONAL PARK
SWAZI-LAND
BASUTO-LAND
0 100 200 300
Scale of Miles
7.

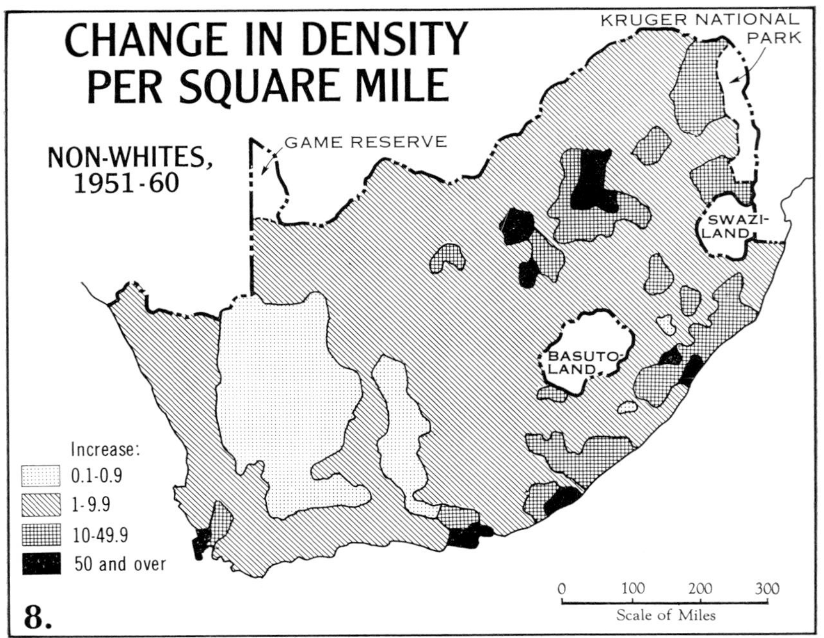
CHANGE IN DENSITY PER SQUARE MILE
NON-WHITES, 1951-60
KRUGER NATIONAL PARK
GAME RESERVE
SWAZI-LAND
BASUTO-LAND
Increase:
0.1-0.9
1-9.9
10-49.9
50 and over
0
100
200
300
Scale of Miles
8.

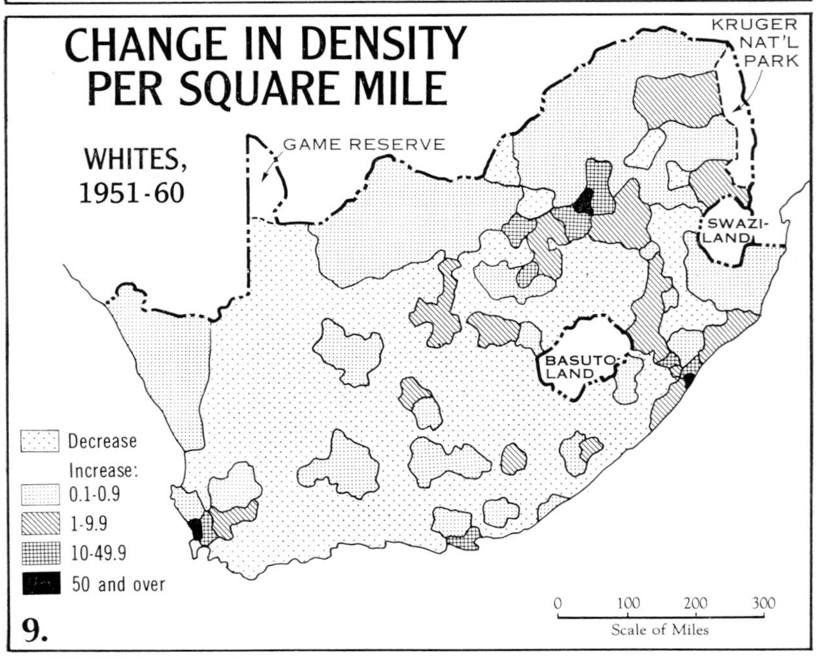
CHANGE IN DENSITY PER SQUARE MILE
WHITES, 1951-60
KRUGER NAT'L PARK
GAME RESERVE
SWAZI-LAND
BASUTO-LAND
Decrease
Increase:
0.1-0.9
1-9.9
10-49.9
50 and over
0
100
200
300
Scale of Miles
9.

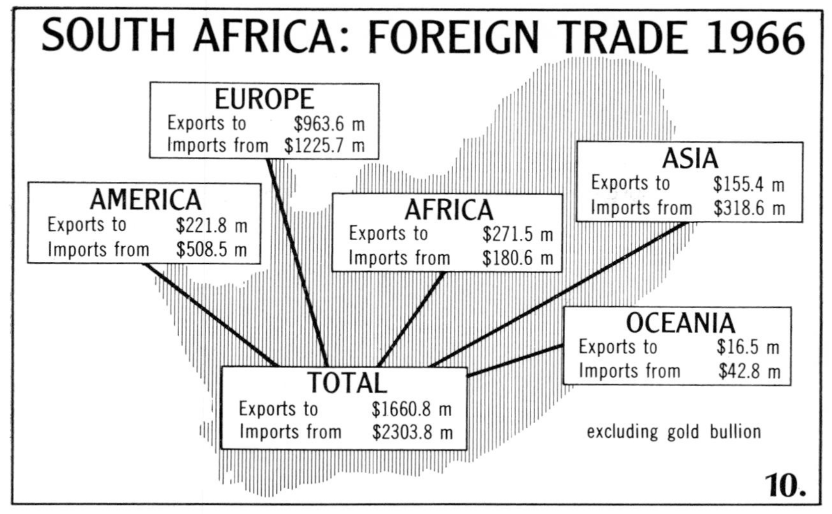
SOUTH AFRICA: FOREIGN TRADE 1966
EUROPE
Exports to $963.6 m
Imports from $1225.7 m
AMERICA
Exports to $221.8 m
Imports from $508.5 m
AFRICA
Exports to $271.5 m
Imports from $180.6 m
ASIA
Exports to $155.4 m
Imports from $318.6 m
OCEANIA
Exports to $16.5 m
Imports from $42.8 m
TOTAL
Exports to $1660.8 m
Imports from $2303.8 m
excluding gold bullion
10.

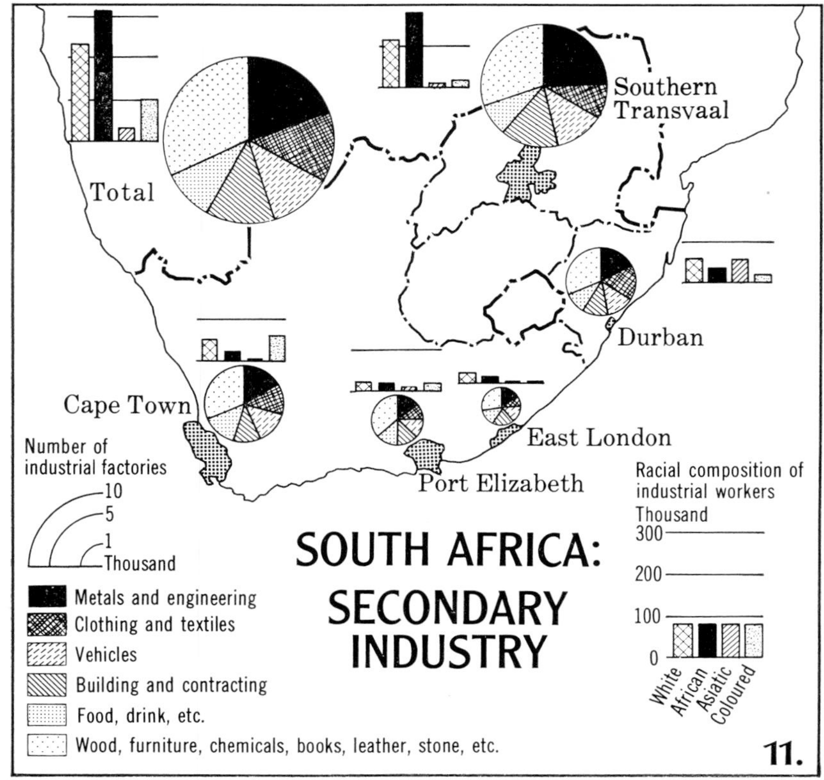
Southern Transvaal
Total
Durban
Cape Town
East London
Port Elizabeth
Number of industrial factories
10
5
1
Thousand
SOUTH AFRICA: SECONDARY INDUSTRY
Racial composition of industrial workers
Thousand
300
200
100
0
White
African
Asiatic
Coloured
Metals and engineering
Clothing and textiles
Vehicles
Building and contracting
Food, drink, etc.
Wood, furniture, chemicals, books, leather, stone, etc.
11.

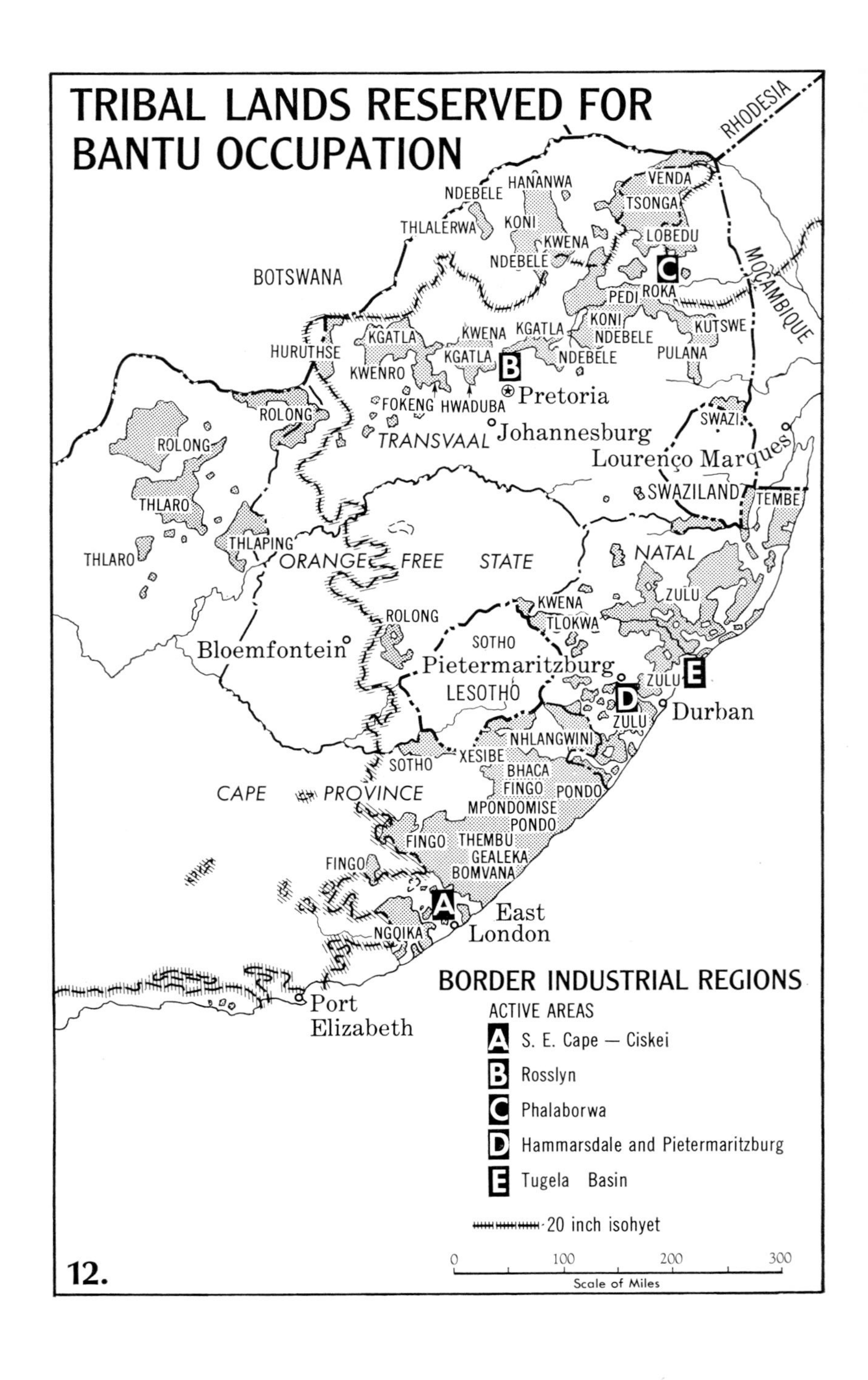

TRIBAL LANDS RESERVED FOR BANTU OCCUPATION
RHODESIA
VENDA
TSONGA
LOBEDU
HANANWA
NDEBELE
KONI
KWENA
THLALERWA
NDEBELE
BOTSWANA
PEDI
ROKA
MOÇAMBIQUE
KOTSWE
KGATLA
KWENA
KGATLA
KONI
NDEBELE
HURUTHSE
KGATLA
NDEBELE
PULANA
KWENRO
Pretoria
FOKENG
HWADUBA
ROLONG
SWAZI
TRANSVAAL
Johannesburg
ROLONG
Lourenço Marques
SWAZILAND
TEMBE
THLARO
THLAPING
NATAL
THLARO
ORANGE FREE STATE
ZULU
KWENA
ROLONG
TLOKWA
SOTHO
Bloemfontein
Pietermaritzburg
ZULU
LESOTHO
Durban
ZULU
NHLANGWINI
SOTHO
XESIBE
BHACA
FINGO
PONDO
CAPE PROVINCE
MPONDOMISE
PONDO
FINGO
THEMBU
GEALEKA
FINGO
BOMVANA
East London
NGQIKA
Port Elizabeth
BORDER INDUSTRIAL REGIONS
ACTIVE AREAS
A S. E. Cape — Ciskei
B Rosslyn
C Phalaborwa
D Hammarsdale and Pietermaritzburg
E Tugela Basin
20 inch isohyet
0 100 200 300
Scale of Miles
12.

FISHING

South Africa is fortunate in having along her coasts two different kinds of ocean, producing different varieties of fish. The Agulhas Waters, extending westward from the Mozambique Channel along the southeast and south coast, are trawled for large edible fish such as hake, sole, and salmon bass, which are distributed as frozen fillets through many African countries, throughout Europe, and in the United States. In addition, tuna, commercially fished by the Japanese long-line method, is exported to Europe and North America. Sharks are also caught by line for their liver oil, their flesh (exported to the Congo), and their fins (exported to China and Hong Kong). Whaling activities center on Durban.

The rich, cold waters of the Atlantic coast, however, account for the greater bulk of fish and fish products. Between Saldanha Bay and Walvis Bay immense shoals of pilchards and mackerel are netted and canned or processed as fish meal and fish oil. Great care is taken to limit the annual catch, the season lasting from January to July, although poachers from other nations pay little heed to such conservation restrictions.

One of the most important exports from South Africa is the rock lobster (clawless crawfish), whose tail forms an effective substitute for true lobster meat. The United States alone imports $12 million worth annually. It is also carefully protected from overexploitation by legal restrictions on size and by seasonal limits. The total annual catch of all kinds of fish places South Africa sixth in quantity among the world's exporters. Recent relaxations of the United States' laws concerning fish meal and its use as a human food when deodorized should stimulate even greater catches of pilchard.

Unfortunately, the South African population does not consume as much fish as many others. The Bantu nations, with few exceptions, have a strong taboo on all forms of fish, regarding them as "serpents." Although industrial workers will happily drink a deodorized fish-meal protein in beverage form and will buy English-style "fish and chips" in a shop, they will not catch the fast-growing carp which are placed in conservation ponds and dams in their reservations, and until habits change, this valuable protein will merely go to waste.

MINERALS AND MINING

Nature has done much to compensate South Africa for its comparatively thin agricultural resources by providing an abundance and variety of minerals, deposited for the most part in the oldest rocks and associated intrusions of the geological column. There are only two instances where the presence of younger rocks would have been an advantage: in petroleum and bauxite, neither of which is found anywhere within the Republic. Numerous past efforts have failed to locate any form of petroleum deposits; however, since 1961, in the face of possible embargoes imposed by the United Nations, the central government has established the Southern Oil Exploration Corporation (SOEKOR) in order to carry out extensive exploration of the Karroo sedimentary beds in the Cape and Natal, and at the same time granting to ten private international and local companies a series of concessions to prospect for natural gas and oil on the continental shelf for three years from 1967 to 1970. There is no confirmation yet of any major reservoirs.

Mineral Shortages. The absence of bauxite has meant that all aluminum used in the Republic is imported from Canada and Great Britain. The possibility of exploiting large deposits of microcline in the eastern Transvaal, containing high fractions of potash and aluminum has been examined. Experimental processing of the low-grade ore containing alumina, based on Russian techniques used in Sakhalin, has also been carried out. While foreign supplies of aluminum are freely available, it is unlikely that costly methods of extraction will be developed merely for the principle of self-sufficiency, although a large alumina smelter is to be built at Richards' Bay, in order to process imported Australian ores.

Apart from oil and bauxite however, it would be difficult to name any minerals which could not be obtained from South Africa in large enough quantities to mine and process for the world's markets. They range from diamonds, platinum, and gold to lowly asbestos.

Diamonds. Diamonds are today extracted in large quantities from the Kimberley and Pretoria kimberlite pipes, with the use of highly sophisticated deep-mining methods, as well as in the traditional manner from river gravels. Materials from raised beaches along the Atlantic, known to contain economic quantities of diamonds, are being mined by adopting "open cast" and dragline techniques. A recent development has been the offshore suction-dredging of gravels lying on the sea bottom along the same coast. As a result, diamond production has steadily increased over the years, although the industry has been warned that if a major discovery is not made during the next 20 years, it will face a serious decline.

South Africa is outmatched in total production but remains the largest producer of gem diamonds by value in the world (Table 13). The parent company, De Beers Consolidated, has also established a Central Selling Organization in London to insure the rational marketing of all gem-quality diamonds. Industrial diamonds, facing imminent competition from synthetically produced stones, find their natural level in world markets. Diamond sales contribute about $45 million annually to the Republic's foreign earnings.

Gold. The presence of gold in southern Africa was known some 600 years ago, and it was mined by early inhabitants of Rhodesia and the Transvaal. Although extracted from the Barberton and Murchison ranges of the eastern Transvaal, it was in the deep basin of ancient rocks (see page 11) in the southern Transvaal that large-scale mining began. Considerable technical skill went into the sinking of deep-level shafts and their ventilation, the blasting, removal, and crushing of hard quartzitic conglomerates, and the separation of a few pennyweights from every ton of ore. Today 45 gold-mining properties stretch in a narrow crescent some 120 miles from west to east of the southern Transvaal. An additional 11 mines now exploit the area of the central Orange Free State, only discovered in 1946. Though they contain exploitable reefs, some of the oldest mines in the central area of the Witwatersrand have been forced to close down in the face of rising production costs against a fixed world price of $35.00 per ounce for gold. Nonetheless more than 33 million ounces are produced and sold either in the London metal exchange or on the open market and provide the Republic with about 42% of its foreign exchange.

TABLE 13

1965 World Production of Diamonds

	In Metric Carats		
COUNTRY	*Gem Quality*	*Industrial Quality*	*Total*
AFRICA			
Angola	878,000	277,000	1,155,000
Central African Republic	268,000	268,000	536,000
Congo (Brazzaville)	318,000	4,982,000	5,300,000
Congo (Kinshasa)	14,000	12,490,000	12,504,000
Ghana	225,000	2,023,000	2,248,000
Guinea	21,000	51,000	72,000
Ivory Coast	116,000	77,000	193,000
Liberia	277,000	263,000	540,000
Sierra Leone	658,000	804,000	1,462,000
Republic of South Africa	1,861,000	2,852,000	4,713,000
South West Africa	1,432,000	158,000	1,590,000
Tanzania	414,000	414,000	828,000
OTHER NATIONS			
Brazil	175,000	175,000	350,000
British Guiana	45,000	68,000	113,000
India	4,000	1,000	5,000
U.S.S.R.	300,000	3,200,000	3,500,000
Venezuela	46,000	45,000	91,000
WORLD TOTAL	7,052,000	28,148,000	35,200,000

Source: Tempo, September 1967, page 5.

Gold profits are subject to special taxation which is used for industrial development, social and welfare programs, and agricultural improvements. It has developed in its wake not only the most advanced mining techniques and research in the world, but also the most powerful educative influence in sub-Saharan Africa. Some 380,000 African workers, about 60% of whom are imported into the Republic as migratory labor, frequently make their first acquaintance with the machine civilization, the shovel, modern hygiene and medicine (including first aid lessons), regular high-quality foods, some degree of literacy, and the ability to use a sewing machine and a boot last. They return with money, goods, and experience to their tribal homes, but seldom stay. Tribal life is disrupted by the absence of these young men, and so begins the first state of the inevitable cultural revolution which Africa must face sooner or later.

Within the South African economy itself the influence of gold mining is incalculable. Around the goldfields has gathered a network of industries which supply stores and machinery of every kind, most of which are manufactured locally. Upon this fundamental base it has been possible to create secondary industries and the manufacture of consumer goods. The total food requirements of this huge regiment of men are important enough to cause a number of adjustments to agriculture. Gold mining also absorbs the largest amount of electricity produced from the country's national power grid. Its tailings created and continue to create the unlovely yellow dumps which sterilize large areas of valuable urban land, but which remind Johannesburg that its dynamic prosperity still rests upon the separation of small quantities of gold from large masses of quartzitic ore.

Uranium as a By-product. While small proportions of silver and other metals make a valuable by-product of the final gold-refining process, it is in the tailings that uraninite is found. Neglected until the arrival of the Nuclear Age, it is now extracted and reduced to inert uranium oxide or yellowcake, from which enriched uranium can be made. South Africa, with 80 years of tailings on the surface and 30 years of gold-reef mining ahead, holds the second largest uranium reserves in the world. Most of the current production of uranium oxide, from 4,000 tons to 6,000 tons, is sold to the British government and Japan. Specialized radioactive isotopes are exported to the United States.

Coal. The known reserves of coal in South Africa are conservatively estimated at more than 80,000 million tons, but many fields have not yet been delineated or evaluated. Present production being about 50 million tons per annum, there is little risk of exhausting supplies for a long time to come. Three major fields—the eastern Transvaal, northern Orange Free State, and northern Natal —supply all the coal required within the Republic and for export. Most of the seams are close to the surface and thick enough to permit the use of mechanical cutters. Some 50,000 Bantu work in the coal mines.

For a number of reasons, South African coal is cheap. Wherever possible, very large thermal power stations are located on or near bituminous yields in the eastern Transvaal and Natal, allowing for the production of cheap electricity (pages 96–98). Anthracite, mined in northern Natal, is being increasingly used in areas where pollution is a serious problem. Unfortunately, there are no large reserves of coking coal for metallurgical coke in the country, but this has been overcome by blending a number of bituminous varieties.

On the northern Orange Free State field, bituminous coals pass directly from the pithead into the vast SASOL plant, which converts it to gasoline, a wide range of distillates, waxes, ammonia, and sulfuric acid. Supplying about 10% of the country's gasoline requirements, this industrial complex is rapidly developing a number of chemical and fertilizer factories around it (page 126).

About 1.4 million tons of coal, principally anthracite, are exported from South Africa to a number of countries. Since the oil-burning ship came into fashion, coal bunkering in Durban has virtually ceased. A new port at Richards' Bay farther north, with direct rail connections to the northern Natal fields, is being constructed in the expectation that some 15 million tons of quality coal will be required in a fuel-deficient western Europe by 1980. In view of its very low pithead prices, South Africa is confident that it can capture large parts of this market, despite the competition of nuclear energy.

Metal Ores. Iron ore is abundant in South Africa. There are some billion tons of high grade ore (65% Fe) 60 billion tons of medium grade, 2 trillion tons of low grade (24–40% Fe) and 2.2 billion tons of titaniferous ores located in the Bushveld Igneous Complex (page 11). Only a few fields are exploited at present—Sishen, Cape Province (which yields about 2 million tons per annum), Thabazimbi, Transvaal (yielding even larger quantities), and northern Natal; but production is rising all the time to meet the demands of growing steel industries in the Transvaal.

The Republic possesses a number of metal ores for the manufacture of ferroalloys. Manganese and chrome deposits are among the world's largest and are exported to most industrial countries, while vanadium has rapidly become an important export concentrate to the U.S.A. There has been in recent years a trend towards local concentration and purification of such additive metals for sale as pure ingots.

South Africa buys all her electrolytic copper from overseas, despite the fact that fair quantities are mined at O'Kiep in Namaqualand and Tsumeb, S.W.A. In the past three years, however, a vast complex has been built in Phalaborwa for extracting more than 100 million tons of blister copper annually from opencast sites. An electrolytic refinery is in process of building, which will handle all the blister copper produced within the Republic and South-West Africa and produce some 45,000 tons of electrolytic copper. Large quantities of magnetite concentrate (8.8 million tons), a by-product of copper production, are being exported to Japan between 1966 and 1967.

Platinum, although rated as a precious metal, has in this electronic age an important industrial role to play. Russian supplies of the metal at one time dominated the world exchanges, but considerable capital investment in northern Transvaal fields will raise production from its present 200,000 ounces to 750,000 ounces, with nickel as a by-product. The bulk of the antimony mined as stibnite in the Murchison Range (page 11) is also exported from South Africa.

Nonmetallic Minerals. In so rich a mineral environment it is not surprising that three major varieties of asbestos are mined for local use and export to Germany, the United Kingdom, and thirty other countries. Vermiculite has also taken its place in the world's market as an insulating material. Among the minerals which have been deliberately sought out are the phosphates, so vital in agriculture. When FOSKOR (see page 126) was established in Phalaborwa, self-sufficiency was assured in the foreseeable future. Limestones, dolomite, and gypsum are abundantly distributed across the country for cement and plasterboard manufacture. Fluorspar and graphite, used extensively in open-hearth furnaces and in the optical industry, are now exported in large quantities to Japan, Australia, Canada, Turkey, Israel, and other countries.

DISCUSSION

From precious stones, semiprecious stones, and precious metals to base minerals, there appears to be no limit to the available raw materials in South Africa. Like most African countries, the Republic until a few years ago preferred to sell most of the base mineral output as crude ore or concentrate. For many years, manganese ore and chromite have been shipped to the United States. Today, these ores can be reduced in bulk by concentration and refining to pure ingots. In the future it is likely that more of this type of conversion will be applied to other mineral ores. In other instances, the mixing of metals with iron to form ferroalloy ingots is already occurring. It has been estimated that by 1975, for instance, 90% of the free world's ferrochrome will come from South Africa. A final state will be reached towards the end of the century when a major part of the production line will remain in the country for processing and conversion to a manufactured object.

POWER AND ENERGY PRODUCTION

Few countries are as favorably placed as South Africa in the matter of coal resources (pp. 93–94). Yet the early stages of the country's development, when coal-field power stations were established in Kimberley and Cape Town in 1882 to meet local demands, actually delayed the progress of thermal power for many years. Until the Transvaal was less sparsely populated, the local coal resources remained in the ground. One of the earliest companies, Victoria Falls and Transvaal Power Company (VFP), was founded in 1906 to bring hydroelectricity from the Victoria Falls, yet it linked up with four thermal stations in Johannesburg with a total generating capacity of 180 megawatts. Similarly, most municipal bodies generated power from small plants to satisfy local demands.

The passing of the Electricity Act in 1922, bringing into being the Electricity Control Board and the Electricity Supply Commission (ESCOM) was a major step towards coordination of power resources, and by 1939 six new stations had been built with a generating capacity of 737 megawatts, and in the nine years following World War II, another came into use, bringing the total capacity of the Commission's stations up to 2,015 megawatts. By the end of 1965 this had increased to 4,175 megawatts generated from 20 stations and for the immediate future enough to satisfy the country's normal requirements.

Emphasis on Thermal Electricity. The need in industrial countries to double electricity production every ten years has not gone unrecognized in South Africa. Vast capital outlay has gone to the construction of four of the world's largest thermal power stations, located in the southeastern Transvaal, and each on its own vast coal field (Table 14). The Commission intends to throw a

TABLE 14

Thermal Power Stations in Eastern Transvaal

Name	*Installed Capacity Megawatts*	*Est. Cost USA $*	*Dressed Coal Consupt. per Ann. (million of tons)*	*Year of Completion*
Komati	1,000	175	5.0	1966
Camden	1,600	196	5.8	1969
Hendrina	2,000	220	7	1970
Arnot (station)	2,100	230	7	1972
Total	6,700	821	24.8	

Source: South African Embassy, Washington.

400-kilowatt network across the country to points as far distant as the northern Transvaal and the western Cape. Now that it has been shown in the United States that high-tension power can be transmitted over long distances (more than 800 miles), it is considered that a hook-up between Camden in the Transvaal and Muldersvlei near Cape Town, a distance of more than 1,000 miles, is feasible, in order to supply the western Cape with cheaper electricity than it could generate locally with imported coals. Power facilities for ten years after 1970 are therefore considered adequate. The only disadvantage appears to be the inability to install the large generating sets now in use in the United Kingdom, owing to the narrow gauge of the National Railroad. Instead of 500-megawatt sets, the Commission is forced to use 200-megawatt sets, a factor offset somewhat by the low price of coal.

Other Sources of Energy. For the decades after 1980 a number of projects have been suggested to supplant local thermal supplies. The first, the Orange River Project (pages 129–132) within its three major dams will supply much of the Cape and Orange Free State with power. More remote in time is the exploitation of the Cabora Bassa area of the Zambezi in Mozambique, 75 miles northwest of Tete, which, with a generating capacity of 2,000 megawatts, can be erected at a cost of $364 million, including the transmission lines. Most of this power could be absorbed by the Republic until it was required in Mozambique.

Central hydrological engineering experts envisage the Okavango River and its swamps as a source of power and irrigation water for South-West Africa, Botswana, and the northwestern Transvaal, if they can be exploited on an internationally cooperative basis. The Cunene River between Angola and South-West Africa is already being dammed for hydroelectric power, but its upper reaches are still untouched. There remain many generating sites on the Zambezi River—the Victoria Falls, Batoka Gorge, Devil's Gorge, and Mpata Gorge as well as Kariba itself—the energy from which could be tapped for those who require it; but these visions do not belong to the present century. Work at Pelindaba, the country's nuclear research center, and experimental trials in a gold mine have demonstrated that nuclear grade uranium oxide can be extracted at less than the present cost of crude uranium exported for refining overseas. Desalination plants with nuclear sources of heat can also be taken a step further and produce electricity. The dry shores of the Atlantic coast could be and probably will be transformed in due course from desert to garden. Work on such a plant is to begin shortly in the Northern Cape.

INDUSTRY AND MANUFACTURE

A wealth of raw materials does not automatically imply a rapid development for any country. Certain conditions appear to be necessary for economic take-off, although disagreement exists among economists as to their precise nature. For South Africa a number of historical, social, and political circumstances appear to have delayed the introduction of full industrialization. As in Spain, physical isolation and distance from the source caused the effects of the European Industrial Revolution to bypass the Cape. Local influences drove the Voortrekker communities even further from any possible contact with the philosophies of industrialism and nineteenth-century radicalism; British colonial policies ensured Cape and Natal docility between 1815 and 1902. After Union in 1910, continued mercantilist philosophies of successive British governments, aimed at providing manufactured goods in exchange for raw materials, postponed for many years any major industrialization program. This suited the mining companies, because all available manpower could then be concentrated in mineral extraction, particularly of diamonds, gold, and coal.

Most important of all influences was the clash between Cecil Rhodes, the creator of the Cape-to-Cairo idea, the personification of enlightened imperialism, on the one hand; and Paul Kruger, President of the South African Republic (Transvaal), representing the distillation of all the Voortrekker desires to be isolated from the main stream in order to live out the biblical analogy of the Israelites' search for the Land of Canaan, the folk myth which had sustained them during their arduous trek. Having found Canaan, Kruger and his *burghers* (citizens) were reluctant to allow Rhodes to spoil it with railroads and aliens. Large-scale gold mining was carried out by *uitlanders* (foreigners) during British suzerainty over the Transvaal (1881–1899), but because such activities ran counter to their rural philosophies, the Boers wanted no part of it except a share in the profits for the Treasury. Failure to abandon this attitude led to the Anglo-Boer War of 1899–1902 (pp. 134–136).

Industrial Beginnings. In reviewing the country's progress since those days, the industrialist Dr. H. J. van Eck pointed out in 1961 how even the most prominent statesmen were influenced by this rural Utopian theme. "An old friend of mine," he said, "met General Botha in Pretoria one evening in 1913. The Union's first Prime Minister was explaining his ideas of land settlement and rehabilitation for the Afrikaner people, but my friend, fresh from the University, had other ideas and suggested that there might be better prospects in commerce and industry. This upset the Prime Minister so much that tears ran down his cheeks at the thought that such a promising young man should have drifted so far from his background as to advocate these revolutionary ideas which were doomed to disaster." The bulk of legislation in the Union Parliament was for the next decade dominated in fact by matter pertaining to agriculture, conservation, irrigation, animal diseases, and land settlement.

The widespread prejudice against trade and industry was also reflected in the absence of Afrikaners from business, industry, and finance when industrial development began in the 1920's. Since World War II, there has been a marked change, however, because large amounts of money held by nationalist and cooperative institutions had to be invested and a new generation of trained men was willing to use it in suitable financial and industrial investments. Whereas in 1930 some 3% of all invested capital in manufacturing enterprises was Afrikaans in origin, by 1965 this had increased to nearly 40%. There are today many thousands of younger Afrikaans executives in every kind of industry and many more, willing refugees from their broken-down utopia, in the lower echelons of mining transport and manufacture. Abandoning the charisma of the nineteenth century has proved a relatively simple process, although the postures adopted by political parties show that rural conservatism remains a powerful force.

The Agricultural Base. Those who advocated industrialization during the decade after union (1910) considered that it should rest primarily on the processing of agricultural produce which, concentrated in the moister Cape area, would make Cape Town the industrial capital of South Africa. This had been, in fact, the general trend of events. The South African Manufacturers' Association was founded in Cape Town in 1904 and launched a "Made in South Africa" campaign in 1907. The first South African Industrial Exhibition, held in 1908, comprised such western Cape products as cheese and butter, flour, wines, brandies, fruit, bacon, carts and wagons, handmade furniture, barrels, boats, soaps and candles, wool, tanned leather and saddlery, tobacco, books, bookbinding, and many other local craft products. In the Transvaal, iron foundries (for machine repairs), an explosives factory, and breweries were merely service industries to the gold mines.

Industrial Expansion. Union of the four provinces in 1910 brought many changes, with the creation of a cabinet post responsible for commerce and industry, and, later, a separate portfolio of mines and industries. Between 1910 and 1914, some 1,600 industries, many protected behind a tariff barrier, were established, chiefly in the Transvaal and Northern Natal, where cement, metal, coke, and power facilities were required for the expanding gold industry. The outbreak of World War I forced South Africa to examine her own resources and to substitute local products for imports whenever possible. By 1920, more than 7,000 factories had been set up, of which 3,000 were located in Cape Province. Automobile fuels from a burgeoning sugar-cane farming industry, leather-tanning material of a local wattle bark extract, and many other import-substitutes were successful until the postwar years 1919–1922, when European trading nations made frenzied attempts to recover their markets. South Africa suffered heavily from overimportation of consumer goods, agricultural depression, stagnating sales, and serious unemployment following the closing of the Kimberley diamond mines, as well as the 1922 Witwatersrand strikes. One major benefit that resulted from these years of depression was a decision on the part of the central government in 1922 that local industries should in the future receive tariff protection from competitors.

Industrial Legislation. Increasing interest in using the country's abundant coal supplies for producing cheap thermal electricity culminated in the formation of the Electricity Supply Commission (ESCOM) in 1923, whose organization and financing methods were to have an overwhelming influence on future patterns of industrial growth (pages 96–98). A series of legislative acts during the next few years—the Industrial Conciliation Act of 1924, the Wage Act of 1925, the formation of a permanent Board of Trade and Industries, and the Customs Tariff Act of 1925—were all evidence of the serious thought given to industrial-manufacturing needs for the future.

Import Substitution. The Customs Tariff Act not only enabled many infant industries to become efficient enough to resist foreign competitors but encouraged the latter to establish their own local factories, thus providing employment within the country itself. General Motors Corporation and Ford Motor Company set up assembly plants in Port Elizabeth, where a rubber tire factory was built soon afterwards. Factories making gasoline pumps, spades, shovels, nails, blankets, hats, boots and shoes, chemicals, soaps, and baking powder followed one another rapidly in various towns. Most of the raw materials and component parts were imported. It has, in fact, taken many years to bring about the next step of using local materials only. Strong incentives now exist, for example, to increase the local content of automobiles, many of which by 1975 are expected to contain no imported components. Powerful lobbying delayed the establishment of an Iron and Steel Industry (ISCOR) on the grounds that it involved governmental capital investment, but it was formally enacted in 1928. It was during this period of prosperity and stability that manganese, Namaqualand diamonds, and Transvaal platinum were discovered. Against strong opposition a local diamond-cutting industry was set up, and the great potential of chromite deposits was noted. The ISCOR iron and steel foundries and coking ovens were built during the World Depression, 1929–32, whose ill effects were softened by South Africa's decision to abandon the gold standard in 1932 and thus encourage foreign capital to invest in the new local industries.

Industrial Breakthrough. When World War II broke out in 1939 the country was well set up industrially, except for the fact that nearly 50% of the raw materials required were imported. In order to survive it was obvious that industries would have to substitute local materials and substitutes. By proving that the latter were satisfactory even by world standards, industry took a vital step forward toward self-sufficiency.

Government interest in all forms of economic development was further stimulated by South Africa's active role in the North African and Middle Eastern theaters of war and her location along a major shipping route to the Far East. Durban and Cape Town became important repair and supply depots as well as manufacturing areas for war materiel. Behind the scenes, General Smuts, the Prime Minister, encouraged his cabinet colleagues, from the outset of this period of unprecedented expansion, to look ahead. One such effort, the Industrial and Agricultural Requirements Commission (1940), led to the appointment of a Social and Economic Planning Council in 1942, which published 14 reports on relevant topics.

Industrial Development Corporation. Reluctance to invest private risk capital in manufacturing industries that were considered to be vital in the future was overcome by the creation by a legislative act in 1940 of a limited company, the Industrial Development Corporation of South Africa (I.D.C.), whose main function was to provide low-interest loans to new but feasible industries and to help existing ones to develop. This act, used in a variety of ways, inspired more industrial progress than any other legislation in the country's history (pp. 123–24). Experience of army contracts during World War II for materials such as footwear, other clothing, and food, placed many of the factories in an unassailable competitive position in postwar years, enabling them to engage in exports on the world markets. Others, less efficient and less conscious of quality, collapsed when deliberately exposed to tariff-free competition.

The industry which benefited most from war-time production was the iron and steel industry. Steel plate mills were set up for armored vehicle construction and ship repairs, rolling mills for rail tracks and structural steel, and special plants for fabricating complex machine parts. All provided excellent experience for the heavy demands of the postwar years.

Modern industry in South Africa has thus accomplished what it was set up to do. The reservoir of skills now available brings every known industry within the compass of the country's desires, from ship-building to nuclear reactors. All types of consumer goods are manufactured locally. Jet aircraft, automobile engines, transistors and electronic equipment (some based on locally invented parts) are now manufactured in South Africa. The government-sponsored Bureau of Standards, a model of its kind, ensures a high standard of quality without which the next step—an export program—could never have been taken. Exports of canned fruits, vegetables, and fish products have been going on for many years, but to these must be added mining machinery, electronic equipment, suits and dresses, shoes, and timber products, all of which are part of a sophisticated competitive world market. Despite political difficulties, these are steadily increasing as new markets such as those in Asia, South America, North America, and the rest of Africa, are tapped.

LOCATION OF INDUSTRY

Not unexpectedly, a greater part of South Africa's industry is located within easy access of the Witwatersrand mining areas which absorb at least 80% of the manufactured capital goods of the country. Seventy per cent of all manufacturing industry is in fact situated in the Southern Transvaal Complex, while 13% and 11% are found in Durban and Cape Town, respectively.

Southern Transvaal Complex. Within the southern Transvaal area is found a greater part of the country's heavy industry. ISCOR in Pretoria, a large steel foundry, has been supplemented by Van der Bijl Park, 60 miles south of Johannesburg, where additional steel is made, and rolling plate and fabricating plants turn out a variety of steels ready for conversion in local factories. Newly erected plants for the preparation of ferroalloys such as ferrochrome and ferrovanadium are also located in the northeastern section of the southern Transvaal zone.

Many factories making consumer products such as soaps have found it necessary to relocate themselves in the southern Transvaal simply because they have discovered their major markets to be there in a community estimated to be some 3,000,000 strong. Railroad freight-charge structure favoring raw materials and penalizing manufactured or processed products have aggravated the position. Regional planners now wonder how much longer this area can be allowed to expand without restriction, in view of the limited water supplies which can be extracted from the Vaal River and its dams. Diversion of Natal rivers or the headwaters of the Orange River in Lesotho has been suggested as a palliative solution, but more drastic measures involving the deliberate decentralization of labor-intensive industries with accompanying incentives have been proposed by the Central Government (pp. 126–27). On the other hand, the building of giant thermal power stations within the area does not suggest that planners expect a serious decline in population or activity in the future.

Although not yet an industrial area, the Orange Free State gold fields will gradually receive industries towards the end of their gold-mining lives. South of Vereeniging, the petrochemical complex of Sasolburg, based on oil extracted from coal, has enticed fertilizer and other petrochemical-based industries to its periphery. A decision to double the size of the oil-from-coal plant immediately carries with it the implication of even greater quantities of coal by-products to be disposed of either locally or as exports.

Natal. Greater Durban is the major entrepôt of South Africa. It is today the country's largest port and performs all the functions of a port: oil bunkering, ship chandling, import-export movements, ship repairs, and ore loading. In addition, a very large sugar refinery exports surplus molasses and sugar. Whaling and fishing have been major industries for many years. In postwar times, refineries have been built south of the city in order to process Middle East petroleum. Grain, wool, and timber are still prominent import-export commodities. Not far from a large graving dock, ship-building yards will soon be completed.

Secondary industry, chiefly food and food processing, has faded into the background of the area's industrial structure. All types of manufacture may now be found within a 20-mile radius, including textiles, aluminum fabrication, furniture, clothing, electronic goods, automobile assembly, and tire manufacture. As industry grows, the old sugar lands to the south of the city have been gradually taken over, first for an international airport, and then as industrial estates. A ferromanganese plant is located near Pietermaritzburg (40 miles inland), close enough for export by sea or to the interior by rail.

The Cape Centers. Cape Town's traditional role as "tavern of the seas" and producer of food products, wines, and fish has always made her a major import-export port. Chilled fruit exports to Europe and North America are loaded in the new harbor. A critical shortage of land has driven industries such as textile, clothing manufacture, and assembly plants, out of the city to more spacious sites on the outskirts.

Port Elizabeth, the principal wool market and entrepôt for Rhodesia, the southeastern region of the Cape known as the Border and the Karroo, acquired a peculiar status back in 1923 by attracting with its cheap land and city taxes two major U.S. automobile assembly plants, Ford and General Motors. These have expanded steadily into adjacent areas such as Uitenhage, attracting tire factories and more recently a carbon-black plant. Government tariff policy is designed to encourage greater use of locally manufactured components until much of the South African automobile can claim to be "local" rather than "imported." This has brought a number of smaller component factories to the city. Large crude ore loading facilities have been erected in the port. Other industries now include leather and tanning, fruit canning, and limestone products.

East London has managed to attract to its river-mouth port a variety of light industries and has recently completed a very large grain-storage elevator chiefly for maize export. It is due to play an increasingly vital role in the government's industrial decentralization policies. Minor centers are Bloemfontein and Kroonstad (railroad centers and rolling stock assembly), Kimberley, and a small cluster of towns in northern Natal based on coal and iron ores. The importance of the latter and of rapidly exploding centers like Phalaborwa in the northeastern Transvaal cannot be overestimated in discussion of future growth in South Africa. Each has the potential to become a major urban complex in its own right.

TRANSPORT SYSTEMS

Large-scale exploitation of any continental interior is generally preceded by early explorations along routes which become well-beaten tracks to favored areas. They are ultimately the routes of the first railroads and highways. Sometimes a river such as the Mississippi will perform a similar function as a penetration route.

In southern Africa rivers have, unfortunately, proved to be unusable for any form of transport. A sandbarred mouth, variable seasonal flow, and the presence of waterfalls deterred easy venture into the interior. Penetration of the subcontinent was achieved by land exploration along routes radiating from Table Bay, across or along the flanks of the southern Folded Mountains on to the plateaus behind them. Many of these became permanent roads along which cattle were periodically driven to Cape Town. Another trackway, remnants of which still survive, was that taken from the eastern Cape by the Voortrekkers' wagon trains as far as the Transvaal and into Natal.

Yet, for all that they were used in the nineteenth century, these pioneer roads were not destined to become the main routes into the interior. Their economic functions were pastoral, leading to rural paradises and political freedom. Those who came after them sought more direct routes to their goal—the diamond diggings of the Vaal River near Kimberley—by using parts of the so-called Missionary Road into Bechuanaland and then turning northeastward. Such journeys were accompanied by ox wagon and lasted several weeks.

Railroads. As elsewhere in Africa, the railroad became the prime method of opening up the interior to mass transportation of goods. Private companies in Durban and Cape Town built short experimental lines by 1860, but the first real service bringing fruit, wheat, and vegetables from the southwest Cape was provided by a 60-mile track between Cape Town and Stellenbosch in 1862. Once the Kimberley diamond diggings had proved to be more than a mere flash in the pan, demand for mining machinery equipment and stores resulted in the rapid extension of the railhead not only from Cape Town but also from Port Elizabeth (Algoa Bay) and East London, both of which could see a rich harvest if they could guarantee quick transport to the northern Cape. Building all three lines proved to be a very difficult engineering task to be undertaken by Colonial governments rather than private companies. The decision to use a narrow gauge throughout (3½ feet) was the inevitable outcome of such physical difficulties and the available steam locomotive power. Substituting a wider standard gauge under modern haulage conditions would today be highly desirable as the country's economy grows, but the cost is considered to be too great.

Once the Escarpment was reached, the Cape Town-Kimberley line was completed by 1885 so that it was possible for the Cape Colonial authorities to link the other two lines at convenient junctions. No attempt was made then or indeed has been made since to connect the three central termini, so that the present-day traveler must still proceed from Port Elizabeth to East London via a junction several hundred miles inland. Building a line from Durban towards the northern Natal coalfields proved to be the most difficult of all the nineteenth-century projects, owing to the steep gradient of all the possible routes between the coast and the Escarpment, so that by 1885 only 180 miles out of a total 300 miles had been covered.

Boer Opposition to Railroads. The opening of the Witwatersrand goldfields from 1886 onwards was immediately reflected in changes in railroad construction policy, for all four coastal towns could now compete for the vast traffic which was bound to result from such an explosive force. The independent views of the two Boer Republics had to be considered, however, causing long delays in the construction of the final links between Cape Town and Johannesburg and in the lines coming from Port Elizabeth and East London via the Orange Free State.

President Kruger's adamant wish to be free of colonial influence held up the entry of the Natal line until a major rail link had been made between Pretoria and Delagoa Bay (Lourenço Marques). His obduracy also prevented Cecil Rhodes from extending his Cape line through the Transvaal into modern Rhodesia. As a result, Rhodes was forced to bypass the Transvaal and to send his railroad through eastern Bechuanaland, yet keeping as close to the Boer republic as possible (much to Bechuanaland's economic disadvantage).

A through line was not made between the Transvaal and Rhodesia and even today does not exist, despite the fact that the respective railheads are little more than 100 miles apart. Rhodesia, in seeking a new outlet to the sea in 1954, chose to perpetuate this policy by building a 400-mile track from Bannockburn to Lourenço Marques.

Major Network. By the turn of the twentieth century, much of the permanent way had been frozen into a transport pattern involving the four major ports directly connected to the Witwatersrand and Kimberley via Mafeking. Thereafter, with only few exceptions, expansion of branch lines was aimed at the more efficient delivery of agricultural products, and more recently, raw materials to the nearest port. Durban, East London, and Port Elizabeth remain unconnected by a coastwise railroad, and in view of the physical difficulties of construction, are likely to remain so for many years to come. The military campaign carried out by Union forces against the German army in South-West Africa in 1914, hinged on the secret construction of a line to carry troops and material in large enough quantities for General Botha to mount a successful action. Since the South-West African gauge was the same, the connection remained a permanent one.

Few new lines have been laid since this great period of expansion. Mileages of open track increased from 7,548 miles in 1911 to 13,098 miles in 1931 and to 13,500 miles in 1965. More attention has been devoted to doubling tracks, in order to avoid the long delays implicit in a single-track system of such great length, and to electrification. Excluding suburban commuter systems, there are today more than 3,000 miles of overhead electric traction lines, more than a third of which are located in Natal. High-powered locomotives are able to use cheap thermal electricity to haul heavy loads from Durban to Johannesburg.

Apart from a short connection from the Orange Free State gold fields to the main line, the only major scheme yet to be undertaken will be that of a line between the northern Natal coal fields and the new port at Richards' Bay in northern Zululand. By directing this route through part of the Tugela drainage basin and the Zulu Homeland (pp. 160–61) the regional planning authorities intend to activate an economically stagnant area of the Republic, while at the same time removing a potential coal-loading burden from Durban, already strained to capacity.

Transport Monopoly. The South African Railway System is efficient although its freight rates leave much to be desired. Changing economic conditions from pioneer farming and mining to industry and manufacture have not changed the physical facts built into the system—long haulage distances, often uneconomic but socially desirable, the peculiarities resulting from the high concentration of people and industries in the southern Transvaal, and many other factors. There have been several official inquiries into the problem, the latest of which will shortly report its findings, but the dilemma is one facing all railroad systems today. The Motor Carriers' Transportation Act of 1930 protects the railroads from their chief rival, the road hauler, who has undermined them in most countries. Road haulage contractors are allowed a larger percentage of the transport market as the problem of getting wide, high loads through rail tunnels between coast and interior becomes insoluble. Nonetheless, official policy, backed by public opinion, requires the ultimate protection of the railroad system.

The railroad service is itself a powerful economic force, employing many thousands of whites and non-whites in maintenance of the permanent way, sidings, and stations. In addition, there are a number of large repair yards and equally important assembly shops where rolling stock of all kinds (including locomotives) is manufactured from South African materials—a result of critical wartime shortages and delays in deliveries from the United Kingdom. It is in this area of railway maintenance that labor shortages have forced a breakthrough in economic integration, Bantu workers being allowed to engage officially in skilled machine work (page 143).

Despite an extensive air passenger service, the railroad remains a popular mode of long-distance travel in South Africa. A number of crack trains for whites and non-white ply between major cities, while others offer a more leisurely trip over many hundreds of miles. More important, however, is the suburban network which carries commuters between home and workplace (Table 15).

Commuter Traffic. Political decisions establishing large non-white townships on the outskirts of large towns (page 140) threw considerable burdens on the rail services which were required to provide regular commuter trains. Of the 400,000 suburban journeys undertaken in 1965, some 219,000 were made in Johannesburg, 102,000 in Cape Town and 38,000 in Durban. Nearly 70% of these journeys were made on third-class tickets, indicating that most of the passengers were Bantu, although a rise of first-class tickets between 1955 and 1965 from 25.6% to 28.1% (Table 15) is partly due to Bantu

TABLE 15

Suburban Rail Traffic in South Africa: Number of Ticket Journeys

Year	*Total*	*1st Class, %*	*2nd Class, %*	*3rd Class, %*
1955	232,723	25.6	19.5	54.9
1965	400,201	28.1	2.4	69.5

Source: Statistical Yearbook 1965.

first-class ticket holders. Many of the peak-hour trains are heavily overcrowded—a problem common to commuter cities—and almost insoluble, except by doubling not only the rolling stock but the rail system as well. There has existed since 1928 an excellent train service between Cape Town and Simonstown alongside which has grown a ribbon of dormitory towns, and between Cape Town and Salt River, carrying a host of the city's industrial workers. Steep gradients have always prevented the growth of similar fast suburban services in Durban beyond a limited range of about ten miles, and consequently this is the area of multiple bus services.

Air Transport. Privately owned commercial air services with a license to carry mail were introduced into South Africa in 1929, but were superseded by a government-sponsored organization in 1934. In such a rapidly expanding economy, internal air travel and air freight services increased very rapidly. In 1964 some 508,000 passengers and 9,400,000 pounds of freight were carried, compared with 131,000 passengers and 484,000 pounds of freight in 1950. All main cities are served at least once daily by the latest jet aircraft while most subsidiary centers are linked with main routes by feeder services. In addition, large numbers of private aircraft are used by businessmen and farmers. Increasing numbers of Indian, Bantu, and Coloured businessmen, chiefs, and politicians are using the National Air Service.

Daily international flights are made by South African Airways to western Europe and the United Kingdom despite a total embargo by most African countries on intermediate stops. From Johannesburg the aircraft flies to Windhoek, Luanda, Las Palmas, and various European capitals. European and U.S. commercial airlines fly regularly to and from Johannesburg. A weekly service to Australia via Mauritius and St. Pauls is shared with an Australian national company. Recent test flights by South African Airways to Latin America and the United States indicate future intentions. Both passenger and freight totals have increased very rapidly since 1950, and despite the enforced detour around West Africa, there seems to be little difficulty in maintaining an efficient and profitable service. Outgoing airfreight consists mainly of valuable materials such as radioactive isotopes (to the United States), diamonds (to western Europe and London), Karakul pelts (for the Italian, German and British fur markets), occasional consignments of gold bullion (to London), and fresh vegetables (to Europe). Incoming freight is made up of badly needed spare parts, specialized machinery, and other general cargo.

Motor Roads and Motor Traffic. The transition from ox-wagon and pony trap to the automobile was made very quickly in South

Africa (Table 16) although mechanization of agriculture itself has been much more gradual. Passenger models were on the roads as early as 1908, and farmers were among the best customers, readily abandoning their sentimental attachment for their oxen in favor of greatly increased mobility. South African dependence on the automobile resembles most closely that of the United States. The car has become a necessity and has steadily reduced the number of public transport services offered by cities except in the non-white sectors where they are still extensively used. The Bantu population owned some 220,000 private automobiles in 1967.

TABLE 16

Motor Vehicles in South Africa

Year	*No. of Automobiles*	*No. of Buses*	*No. of Commercial Vehicles*	*No. of Motorcycles*
1920	24,064	115	905	14,924
1950	471,374	4,433	123,549	23,859
1965	1,015,000	18,000	243,000	90,000

Sources: Union Statistics for Fifty Years 1910–1960 and Department of Information, South Africa.

In 1916 there were 47,000 miles of highway, only a tiny fraction of which were paved. By 1964 there were 14,306 miles of tar-macadamized road surface out of a total of 115,600 miles of main highway. In view of their high costs, paved roads had to wait for a coking industry and, more recently, the oil-from-coal industry, to supply tar at economical prices.

As early as 1935 a National Road System was initiated, financed by gasoline import taxes and government funds. In the hands of provincial authorities the arterial highways connecting all the metropolitan areas are being standardized to conform to a number of requirements, not the least of which is the widening or construction of bridges. To cope with the phenomenal increase in automobiles and buses, cities such as Johannesburg, Cape Town, and Durban have undertaken extensive highway programs which, together with the national network, make South Africa, in the words of a highway expert "the only country in the world where roads are ahead of the traffic." Considering the increase in vehicle numbers which is bound to come as general standards of living rise, it will be interesting to see how long this statement remains valid. A Japanese auto-assembly plant in a Border Industrial Area near Pretoria has set aside some 5,000 places in its parking lot for its Bantu employees who will be buying cars during the next ten years.

Shipping. There are no natural harbors around the South African coastline. Historic shipwrecks in Table Bay and False Bay offer abundant evidence of the dangers of what appear to be the safest harborages. Durban is a man-made harbor dredged from a silted lagoon. All South African harbors are in fact artificially constructed to cope with heavy persistent swell and high winds. Considerable sums have been spent on renovating the four major ports in order to accommodate heavy import and export traffic, and with the inevitable decline of the Suez Canal, to cope with new shipping trends.

Shipping services were until a few years ago mainly in the hands of foreign companies. British lines provided a fast and regular mail, passenger, general, and refrigerated cargo service between the United Kingdom and South African ports, while Japanese, German, French, and Italian companies called regularly. Small coastal vessels plying between a number of estuary ports, most of which have long since died from silting-up, have also declined in number as the center of economic gravity has shifted to either the Transvaal or the major ports.

A South African Merchant Marine. There has been an important change in the last five years in the Republic's attitude towards a merchant marine. Assisted by the Industrial Development Corporation, SAFMARINE (see page 125), a local company group, has purchased a number of passenger ships and is adding by new construction a fleet of cargo and refrigeration vessels, and by charter several oil carriers. Inspired in part by fear of international political repercussions, but mostly by simple economic self-interest, it has also decided to set up a ship-building industry in Durban and Cape

Town. There are now registered under the South African flag some 24 foreign-going ships, consisting of two passenger liners, twelve general cargo, two bulk pig-iron carriers, one 77,000 ton and two smaller oil carriers. By 1970 SAFMARINE is expected to have an operating fleet of 35 ships, placing the country in a sound maritime position to export and import goods in her own bottoms.

5 *Patterns of Economic Growth*

It should be evident that South Africa's economic position, by world standards, is a very stable one. This can be partly attributed to the use of firm budgeting and financial controls during periods of threatened inflation. More important, however, is the fact that gold bullion is a major item in the export list, differing from other items in that its selling price has by international agreement remained at a fixed level of $35.00 per troy ounce since 1934.

During boom periods when commodity prices and production costs are rising, the gold producers, unable to raise their prices, are therefore forced to reduce their profit margins, thus taking considerable amounts of money out of circulation. During a recession, lowered costs will correspondingly make more money available. Alternatively, if a central government were to allow costs to rise disproportionately, so narrow is this profit margin that most gold mines would be forced to close down. Not only would there be large numbers of men unemployed but every sector of the economy would be affected.

Caught between Scylla and Charybdis, no South African government can afford to create fluidity by the simple act of inflation and increased paper currency. It must be constantly on guard for signs of overheating in the economy and ready to intervene. Certain benefits flow from this situation, however. The South African gold mines are highly efficient, seeking on the one hand ways to reduce costs and on the other hand ways of increasing the productivity of workers. Technical training and education therefore play an important part in gold-mining organizations, reaching down as far as the humblest migrant laborer.

In external trade, gold is also a desirable item of exchange for any country selling capital goods to South Africa. The government, though entitled to do so, seldom used this device, preferring to dispose of most of its gold production through official channels in London in exchange for currency. Attempts by the United States to displace gold as an international currency have resulted in a rapid change of policy. There is, however, a limited life of twenty to thirty years for most of the mines, some of whose reefs are already being abandoned because they are uneconomical to process. Only the presence of uranium ores permits certain others to be used for gold extraction.

This prospect, however dismal, was in fact, foreseen some 45 years ago. It was possible to create a manufacturing industry which, protected behind a tariff, grew from tender infancy to its present-day lusty adolescence. The next stage in economic growth therefore implies a gradual replacement of gold by manufactured goods for export, in a jungle of intensely competitive trading nations. Politically inspired embargoes and trade boycotts have signally failed to prevent the rapid expansion of trade between South Africa and many industrialized countries such as France, Italy, Spain, West Germany, and Japan as well as its traditional and oldest trading partners, the United Kingdom and the United States. Considerable trading links have grown with the rest of Africa since 1961.

Direction of Trade. South Africa's best trading customer is the United Kingdom, even if gold is excluded from consideration. In 1966 South Africa exported $537 million worth of goods to the United Kingdom, mainly in the form of primary agricultural products, canned fruit and vegetables, fish, meat, and a variety of metals, all of which represented 30% of the country's exports. The United Kingdom, in turn, exported about $760 million worth of manufactured goods consisting mostly of machinery, transport equipment, automobiles, and many other products.

Second to the United Kingdom, the United States received about 250,000,000 dollars' worth of South African imports, mainly minerals and fruits, in 1966, and exported about $450 million worth consisting of machinery, spare parts, and specialized dollar goods. Growing exchanges with France, West Germany, Switzerland, Spain, Italy, and certain African countries have not lessened the powerful symbiosis of South Africa with the United Kingdom, although this is likely to weaken should the latter find a place in the European Common Market. Outside this area, Japan has offered considerable markets for South African anthracite, sugar, wattlebark, and magnetite as well as a great variety of agricultural products. In return, South Africa has received quantities of machinery, electronic equipment, textiles, clothing, iron and steel, scientific instruments, and petroleum products, most of which had been the prerogative of the United Kingdom in past years.

Increasing Exports. Despite boycott campaigns on the part of a number of Afro-Asian nations, exports have continued to grow in the past five years to Asia and the rest of Africa. Most of these consist of processed foods, mining machinery, and clothing, which frequently go to a British port for relabeling before being sent to their African destinations. South Africa has also become an important trader with Zambia, displacing Rhodesia, which is now under the cloud of an embargo. Aggressive trade missions are seeking new markets in the Far East, South America, Canada, Australia, and Africa, not only for primary agricultural products but also for capital goods such as mining machinery, tools, fabricated steel and other metals, textiles, clothing, chemicals, processed foods, and tobacco. Quality, rigidly controlled by the Bureau of Standards, and delivery on time appear to be the most attractive features of South African sales programs, while the establishment of credit facilities through industrial credit banks, and "most favored nations" trade agreements with Spain, France, and Italy have enabled exporters to penetrate protected markets.

The economic picture in South Africa is therefore changing so rapidly that it has proved impossible to judge future trends with any certainty. Quickening foreign demands for diamonds, uranium, ferrochrome, manganese, electrolytic copper, platinum, vanadium, and asbestos are likely at some time in the next decade, and, failing mandatory sanctions, South Africa is able to supply all of them. Maize, fruits, lobster tails, fish, and fishmeal will always be in demand in a hungry world which is growing hungrier. A market for increasing surpluses of paper-pulp timber and petrochemicals will have to be found, too.

At the same time, internal markets are expanding, particularly among the non-white communities, whose domestic spending power has grown astonishingly in the past ten years. It has been estimated that by the year 2000, Bantu spending power alone will have risen from its present $1.7 billion to at least $6 billion per annum, to be spent on consumer goods such as household equipment, clothing, automobiles, liquor, most of which will undoubtedly be manufactured locally.

Foreign and Domestic Investment. Some 22 countries in 1964 represented more than 70% of the total foreign investment in South Africa, which amounted to $4,480 million in 1965. Of this total, some $2,622 million was held by the United Kingdom which, despite changes in political affiliations, has always found gold, diamond, and mineral extraction an excellent investment. This has been supplemented by vehicle assembly plants, factories, and textile mills in the years since World War II. Compared with an average annual return of 10.6% from the sterling area in 1963, South African investments yielded 15.3% net.

For the United States, South Africa represents the "most profitable country for private investment in the world." Gross yields were 17.1% (15% net) in 1963 on a direct investment of $504 million. There are now 243 United States' companies operating within the Republic.

Evidence of growing European interest is indicated by business investment from France ($245 million), Switzerland ($194 million), and Germany ($80 million), whose holdings are in local factories and plants in order to avoid tariff and import duties.

Local investment funds are considerable, and with few exceptions are used locally for capital formation. Only in recent years have areas like Bermuda and Australia been used for specialized company formation. One of the elements in this funding process has been the remarkable flow of capital from Afrikaans cooperative organizations, insurance companies, and banks, which, when founded in the 1930's, saw little virtue in investing in "English" companies. This important change of attitude on the part of Afrikaans-speaking people has deep political implications, in that if falling incomes are at any time due to unmanned machines in factories, then men will have to be found to work them, be they black, white, or khaki! Such financial considerations are likely to break down "racial" barriers in industry more rapidly than any other single factor.

A Common Market? In considering ways of expanding trade, some South African economists envisage the forming of a Common Market comprising all ten countries of "Southern" Africa (south of the Congo-Zambezi divide). There are valid reasons for such a step. South Africa has invested considerable sums in neighboring territories; its own mines and industries provide work wages, and therefore foreign exchange, for more than a million foreign African migrants, who send back between 30% and 60% of their earnings to their homelands; South Africa sells large quantities of machinery, food, clothing, and manufactured goods to all of these territories and is in a position to supply technical aid at any time.

A successful Common Market, however, relies upon the fact that all its member economies are roughly at about the same level. Unfortunately, the disparate rates of economic development of the ten countries mitigate against any closer association in the foreseeable future. It is more likely that comprehensive bilateral agreements will provide the first economic linkages, one of which has existed for many years with Rhodesia. Trade pacts were recently signed with Malawi and in a modified form with Lesotho. Angola and Mozambique, slowly escaping from the restrictive mercantilist policies of their mother country, are bound sooner or later to seek similar agreements. At present, Zambia, despite a large trade with South Africa, appears to be moving away from the southern watershed towards East Africa.

THE TECHNIQUES OF INDUSTRIAL AND ECONOMIC DEVELOPMENT

The Problem. When developing countries offer incentives to encourage industry, they invariably find that investors prefer industries which have guaranteed markets, easy profits, and minimal risks. The resulting imbalance in favor of quick-selling consumer goods thus defeats the fundamental need to establish the new industries most needed. The solution to this problem often turns out to be socialism or planned intervention by the government.

Government Sponsorship. In South Africa, private enterprise has provided the bulk of invested capital for industrial development. The funds and skills necessary for filling vital gaps in the economic structure have, however, been provided by government-sponsored development corporations which have been adapted for use in a number of situations. A characteristic example is found in the Bantu homelands (page 160), where capital starvation would hold back any form of economic development in the community. Though such corporations have taken various forms, from outright national ownership to shareholding capitalist enterprises, they all have one particular policy in common: since each was created to provide service to the total community, none is permitted to show conspicuous working profits; these must be ploughed back into investment or used to lower prices.

Public Utilities. Accordingly, the South African Railways and Harbors, wholly national since Union, is obliged to provide transport services as widely as possible on a commercial basis. In return, the Board is guaranteed a near-monopoly on the carriage of all goods, enabling it to offer important road-feeder services from all railroads without fear of competition from private road traffic. Ports, harbors and airways are similiarly controlled by the central authority. In a country so large and yet with so small an economic population, this type of development has proved to be an advantage, in that wasteful competition for capital has been avoided. The danger of interference, mostly through political nepotism, was present for a short period after World War II, but this has been dissipated by strict observance of the commercial character of the system. Consequently, railroad, bus, air, and harbor services are efficiently run, and considerable thought is given to planning future capital investment and expansion.

The same may be said of the Electrical Supply Commission (ESCOM), which was established in 1922. From pioneer experiments with pulverized coal fuel, this Commission has created a series of power grids across the country, based on very large thermal stations located as close to a coalfield as possible. Because it is required to supply electricity without profit or loss, unit prices are among the world's lowest—an important factor in a country almost devoid of hydroelectric power. It has thus been possible, by extensive building programs, to keep pace with the demands of mining, industry, and growing urban communities, and within 10 years power supplies will have doubled (pages 97–99).

A badly needed national policy toward water resources and requirements has only begun to emerge from such bodies as the Resources and Planning Advisory Council. Competition for water in the Transvaal, first for industry and next for new thermal power stations, has reached the saturation point, forcing the planners to look further afield for assured supplies (pp. 128–30). Desalination of seawater for coastal cities from plants fueled by nuclear energy is considered to be a necessity from 1990 onwards.

Iron and Steel Industry. Another quasi-state body is the South African Iron and Steel Corporation (ISCOR), which passed into government hands when nearly all the issue of 6,000,000 ordinary shares failed to attract the general public in 1928. The central authorities were thus forced to take them up, against loud vocal opposition from British and European steel exporters, whose guaranteed and highly profitable market in South Africa looked like disappearing—a fear since wholly justified. The Corporation has expanded remarkably in the past 20 years, offers cheaply priced steels and pig iron of excellent quality to local and export markets. New patented furnace techniques, methods of preventing rust on structural steels, and advanced research facilities have placed the industry in the forefront of steel technology. By world standards production is slight—about 4,000,000 tons a year—but there are plans for unrestrained expansion in the future.

Other Investments. Smaller state corporations such as the Fisheries Development Corporation (FISHCOR) and Klipfontein Organic Products Corporation (KOP) were established during World War II with specific aims in view. The former, activated in 1944, was intended to put commercial fishing on a rational basis, but its functions went far beyond that aim. Boat and housing loans, water and electrical supplies, new shipways and ports, fish-oil storage plants, and sponsoring of research have been added to the original marketing and organizational programs. The Klipfontein plant (KOP), a chemical warfare factory throughout World War II, was due to be closed in 1945 but was converted to insecticide manufacture, all of which was used to combat typhus epidemics in war-torn Europe, and later to drive the tsetse fly and mosquito away from a million acres of good ranching land in northern Natal. When locust plagues struck south and central Africa in 1962 and 1963, cheap KOP insecticides were immediately available for aerial spraying.

INDUSTRIAL DEVELOPMENT CORPORATIONS

The South African Industrial Corporation (IDC) differs from its stablemates in function and purpose. It is a limited company which came into being by an Act of Parliament on May 15, 1940, to "constitute a corporation the object of which shall be to promote the establishment of new industries and industrial undertakings and to provide for other incidental matters." With a nominal capital of 5 million Rand ($7 million dollars) and a Board of Directors from which all members of the government were excluded, it began its career by offering R3,000 ($4,200) to a struggling food manufacturer to enable him to survive his early difficulties and make good. In 1942 the enabling act was amended in order to allow the corporation to widen its functions by including the establishment and operation of any industrial undertaking it deemed essential to the country's economic welfare. Armed with these new powers, IDC moved into an expanding field of research, investment, technology, and management in South African industry by initiating manufactures for which there seemed little demand under contemporary world trading conditions. A model of its kind, the corporation has been responsible for accelerating an industrial revolution, stimulating the private sector to greater efforts and creating a suitable atmosphere for foreign investment.

The Directors of IDC were and remained generally modern

technocrats, highly qualified, pragmatic, and apolitical. Investment earnings are slight, mainly because many ventures require about eight years before they show any realistic profit. Modest reserves have been slowly accumulated, and whenever it is considered that an industry can stand on its own feet, the corporation's portfolio is disposed of in the stock exchange. During the financial year ending June 30, 1966, 916 enquiries about financial assistance had been submitted, 286 were investigated in terms of strict feasibility requirements and 97 were accepted, involving new commitments of R62.5 million ($87.5 million). Since its inception, the corporation has accepted propositions with a gross value of R433 million ($606.2 million), and its own investments are valued today at R326 million ($456.4 million).

Types of Industrial Investment. In favoring certain types of industry, the IDC placed great emphasis on those which are labor-intensive, consume large amounts of cheap power, utilize local raw materials hitherto untouched or exported without processing, process foods and thus reduce wastage while stabilizing prices, and finally, appear to have expanding market capacities as the population increases. The textile industry was best qualified to meet these requirements, with the result that IDC entered into financial partnership with prominent textile firms in Great Britain in order to set up cotton mills in Kingwilliamstown and East London, and a fine worsted woollen factory near Port Elizabeth. Fifteen textile establishments have succeeded not only in local markets but also in markets of many overseas countries.

Food processing of perishable dairy products into cheese, butter, powdered milk, and animal feeds came next, after which the corporation set about persuading timber companies and their associates to set up hardboard and kraft paper mills, using local wattle wood. A major success was recorded when the firm of Courtaulds of Great Britain was persuaded to set up SAICCOR (South African Industrial Cellulose Corporation), a large rayon-from-pulp industry in Natal, based on fast-growing salignum gum and pine plantations. A more recent achievement has been the creation of a nylon spinning factory in the southwest Cape Province.

There are few areas of manufacture which have not experienced the energetic stimulation of IDC. It has brought paints, cables, cranes, steel presses, farm implements, concrete pipes, cardboard containers, footwear, and a variety of chemicals to a country which had not considered it worthwhile to make them. Since there is no restrictive monopoly involved, industrialists have been quick to learn the possibilities of the local and foreign markets.

Other projects in which IDC is deeply involved are jet aircraft construction, ship-building facilities, the South Atlantic Cable (between Cape Town and London), oil exploration (SOEKOR), a South African merchant fleet (SAFMARINE), tea-growing ventures (SAPEKOE), a carbon-black factory, china and porcelain, and cement and lime. It has recently been decided, after long negotiations with foreign producers and detailed feasibility studies, to underwrite an aluminum smelter to the tune of R35 million ($49 million).

In the field of automobile assembly, powerful incentives have been offered in order to hasten a car of South African origin by setting up local component factories, erecting a body-pressing plant, and making a diesel engine. Here the problem of location makes it difficult to reconcile auto assembly in Port Elizabeth with a pressed body having to come from the southern Transvaal. The former is permanently fixed at a seaport to receive disassembled automobiles from the U.S.A. and would find a move to the market extremely costly. Nonetheless, increased local content is likely to come about simply because the IDC has taken the initial steps.

Other Interests. IDC is active in South-West Africa with SWAWEK, a water supply corporation, while in recent years it has created ancillary financial services in the Republic for industries ambitious to export their skills or goods. An accepting bank for industry, a national discount house, and an export credit finance scheme all enable industrialists to fulfill contracts in France, Italy, and Spain without the difficulties usually associated with absence of credit. Neither have small industries been neglected; 42% of all applications that have been granted for sums less than R50,000 ($70,000) have come from a special division of the corporation.

Self-Sufficiency Programs. Taking into account the possible effects of an international economic embargo against the South African government, the IDC performed its most important work in establishing an oil-from-coal corporation (SASOL) in the northern Orange Free State. This supplies the country with 10% of its gasoline requirements and a vast surplus of petrochemicals and gas, all of which have been put to good use. A special gas corporation now pipes gas to the Witwatersrand area, while from coal, air, and water comes a great complex of chemical manufactures. A total of R112 million ($157 million) was spent on this project, and in view of the technical snags encountered throughout the construction of the plant, it must be considered the kind of high risk investment which only IDC could underwrite. It has proved so successful, however, that the entire complex is to be doubled in size immediately; furthermore it has stimulated a number of United States petroleum companies to buy up many Illinois coalfields with similar ends in view.

Yet another major investment (R18 million) sponsored by IDC which has proved itself, was the Phosphate Development Corporation (FOSKOR), whose object was superphosphate self-sufficiency, from large deposits at Phalaborwa in the Transvaal. Having helped to mobilize most of the capital for erecting the Palabora Mining Company's copper extraction plant, IDC can claim to have created a vast new industrial complex yielding superphosphates, magnetite (exported to Japan), copper and copper concentrates, zirconium, and vermiculite, to be followed shortly by an electrolytic copper refinery with an annual capacity of 45,000 tons now under construction.

Decentralization of Certain Industries. The technocrats of the Industrial Development Corporation are in favor of decentralization of industry wherever possible, and the fact that this coincides with the official government policy of separate development, has led to the very rapid growth of the so-called border industrial regions, situated as close to the Bantu homelands as possible in order to offer employment to Bantu adults who otherwise would be forced to make the migrant journey to the distant cities (pp. 163–66). Considerable controversy has surrounded the border industrial concept, mainly on the grounds that it disperses the concentrated energies of the major industrial zones; but, attracted by strong incentives, many labor-intensive industries have moved into such areas with the investment support of IDC.

IDC and Homeland Development. Finally, the idea of the state-sponsored corporation has proliferated among the various ethnic groupings of the country. From the mother corporation have been spawned a Bantu Industrial Development Corporation, a Bantu Investment Corporation, and most recently, an Indian Development Corporation and a Coloured Development Corporation. All have the same kind of constitution as the original. All are designed on the one hand to offer loans, investment funds, and technical advice to those who wish to start or expand industries and businesses, and on the other to provide an opportunity for people to invest their savings in an organization which will pay interest and use the principal to develop local enterprise. Despite many early doubts on the part of some experts, the basic idea has been enthusiastically received and gradually translated into reality.

LONG-TERM ECONOMIC DEVELOPMENT PLANS

National economic planning in South Africa has until recently been confined to the conservation of resources, regional planning of various strategic areas, and political relocation of populations. Though these plans were well executed, most took little note of the total socioeconomic perspective. Aware of this weakness, the Prime Minister's Economic Advisory Council produced South Africa's first Economic Development Plan for the years 1964–1969 in December 1964. A second plan, for the years 1965–70, published in December 1965, showed that severe inflationary pressures were endangering the prosperity of the agricultural and mining industries as a result of an annual growth rate of the gross national product of 8%, second in the world to Japan's 10%. The decision to peg this rate to 5.4% was intended not only to curb inflation but to keep pace with growth of the available labor force, its education and training. The main conclusions of the EDP, in fact, concern the growing shortage of skilled labor which will be required to cope with a 5% growth rate despite an annual immigration of 40,000 Europeans—a matter of some political significance which is already influencing white trade-union attitudes towards using Bantu as skilled workers, in itself a major permissive breach in *apartheid* legislation.

In 1967 the government went one step further by enacting a law concerned with overall planning. The Physical Planning and Utilization of Resources Act, regarded with deep suspicion by the parliamentary opposition as yet another restrictive device, does nevertheless embody valuable long-range planning concepts. Its main purpose is to prevent the needless waste of physical resources and too haphazard a growth of the country's socioeconomic life.

WATER AS A PLANNED RESOURCE

Like most other countries, South Africa has had to examine its present and future water requirements for a population which will have grown from 18 million in 1966 to a possible 42 million by the year 2000, with a natural concentration of nearly 75% east of the 20-inch isohyet.

Water Shortages. It has been known for some time that the Vaal River can no longer satisfy the demand of the southern Transvaal complex, despite the construction of several new dams along its course. A number of schemes have been suggested to swell the available water supply coming into the Vaal dam. Among these is the Oxbow Scheme, designed to make fuller use of the considerable head of water on the upper Malimbamatso River in northern Lesotho by the building of a high dam which would increase supplies to the southern Transvaal by 30%. Another involves a neighboring river, the Kau, which would probably raise the total reserves by 75%. Yet another scheme involving the diversion of one or more of the perennial Natal streams on the eastern flank of the Drakensberg Escarpment is receiving serious analysis. How best to utilize the excellent water supplies from the Tugela has engaged the close scrutiny of regional planners for the past twenty years. Paper and rayon mills have been situated close to the mainstream, dams are being built in the upper reaches and major tributaries in the expectation that the important coal, iron, and steel industrial complex of northern Natal and ultimately the Zulu homeland will continue to expand and require much larger quantities of industrial water.

Such then is South Africa's water problem—abundant water is available but not in the places where it can easily be used. The Vaal-Caledon-Orange system is the only significant westward-flowing one across the interior. All other major streams such as the Olifants, Pongola, Tugela, Fish, and Kei flow eastward from the escarpment edge to the Indian Ocean, and through normally perennial, flow swiftly through drought-free areas which are, however, too steep and rugged for cultivation and irrigation. For the national planners, the prospect of a country heavily loaded with people on its eastern side while usable land lies empty over much of the remaining two-thirds,—and watered land, though watered by seasonal, erratically flowing rivers—is not a healthy one, particularly in the light of future demographic trends and food needs.

The Orange River Project. After many years of background research a thirty-year plan for bringing the waters of the Orange River Basin under control was published in 1962. Known as the Orange River Project (ORP), it envisaged the contruction of dams, hydroelectric stations, pipelines, canals, and irrigation channels in order to rejuvenate and develop a very large semiarid area extending from the southeastern Cape to the barren shores of South-West Africa, where minor irrigation schemes such as those at Upington and Kakamas have shown the considerable irrigation farming potential of such a river.

The Project has been subdivided into six phases of development. The first, covering a five-year period, involves the erection of two major holding reservoirs—already named the Hendrik Verwoerd and the Van der Kloof dams—in the upper middle course of the river. These have an immediate urgency, since they will provide water for the growing urban and industrial centers of Bloemfontein and Kimberley as well as the Orange Free State gold-mining complex, which is itself destined to become industrialized. The excavation of a 51-mile tunnel from the Hendrik Verwoerd damsite southwards will break through the Orange Divide to that of the

Great Fish River and revive the irrigated lands of the Fish, Breede, and Sundays valleys, where failing water supplies and drought have sharply reduced the production of citrus fruits and killed many trees. Irrigation canals will also carry water to reinforce the Vaal-Hartz Irrigation Scheme and to open up new lands west of Kimberley as far as the west coast to irrigation agriculture.

The second phase, lasting some five to ten years, involves the building of a third major dam in the middle course—the Torquay Dam—as well as the creation of a network of hydroelectric stations along the middle and lower courses to provide energy for pumping water and industrial undertakings in the northern Cape, southeastern Cape, and southern Orange Free State—all areas where coal would be too expensive for conventional power stations. In the four remaining phases, spanning some twenty years, further irrigation canals will be cut, and water will be directed to smaller towns such as Graaf Reinet, Cradock, and De Aar and to the major industrial center of Port Elizabeth, whose domestic water supplies will be inadequate for continued growth despite the completion of the Kouga Dam about eighty miles away. The remaining hydroelectric stations will also be built. When the scheme is complete, some twenty hydroelectric stations will supply 117 megawatts for local and regional use, while some 756,000 acres will be irrigated. The total cost over thirty years is estimated at about $1,200 million, which is being raised locally or through French banks.

Progress. The scheme has gone far beyond mere conjecture. Work has been completed on the contractors' bridges at the dam-wall sites, while trial-shaft sinking has been carried out on the line of the Orange-Fish Tunnel. All preliminary geological testing of the bedrock and quarry materials for aggregate has been accomplished. Contracts for all construction, concrete, and drilling operations have been signed with a consortium of South African and French firms whose joint skills are best suited to this kind of work. Most of the earth-moving machinery will be constructed in South Africa, while most of the executive work will be in the hands of South African engineers. Bantu labor has been deliberately recruited from areas of high unemployment such as Zululand. Fully equipped townships have already been laid out and constructed for all workers. Intensive geological, archaeological, and other scientific field work is being carried out with government support, in the "flood" areas, while social scientists and agroeconomists have surveyed present land use, population distribution, and socioeconomic conditions with a view to predicting probable settlement and economic development patterns between 1970 and 1995.

The Orange River Project is a bold, imaginative scheme, as ambitious as that of the Tennessee Valley Authority, and designed to effect similar environmental changes. Since electrical power and water supplies are already public utilities in South Africa, there is no likelihood of conflict with private enterprise. Vast areas of irrigable land will be available by 1990 to guarantee sufficient wheat, cotton, and other crops at present imported to meet local demands, enough lucerne (alfalfa) to supply not only the dairy and beef industries of the entire country but also to feed a growing sheep population, a million of which now die annually from starvation. Furthermore, new plantings of deciduous and citrus fruits as well as vegetables will add to the country's domestic food supplies as well as to the export market.

It is too early to say whether the catchment area between Kimberley and Alexander Bay will attract industrial undertakings (except canning and allied processing plants) in sufficient numbers to meet the planners' current optimism, but guaranteed water supplies, combined with the invariably sunny climate, could well revolutionize the area. Among the scheme's most vital, yet unpublicized, functions will be the containment of the Karroo scrub vegetation, whose pioneering and colonizing propensities have for 75 years been a continuous threat to the grassland (*veld*) of the Orange Free State, the southeastern Cape, and Natal as overgrazing, burning, and drought encouraged its advance.

Critical Comment. Criticism has been concentrated on detail rather than the general principle. Few experts deny the need for a westward extension of settlement, although some would consider the further decentralization of industry a regressive step in the development of the country as a whole. Others have asked whether sufficient manpower will ever be available to practice the skilled art of intensive irrigation farming on so vast a scale. Climatologists have pointed to the danger in a semiarid region of continuous, excessive evaporation and rapid salt concentration near the soil surface, a process which has led to the abandoning of hundreds of acres of irrigated land annually in California. Some economists have questioned the country's ability to absorb the amount of food which would be available by 1995 if all goes as planned and have seriously questioned the amount of capital required to complete all phases of the scheme.

Most serious of all the difficulties is that of accumulating silt from the Upper Orange watercourse. Although the engineers have designed the Verwoerd Dam wall so that it can be raised at regular intervals in order to maintain water depths in the foreseeable future, the fundamental problem remains that of stabilizing the landscape of the basin itself. Planned land use, conservation practices, and watershed protection are urgently required in Lesotho. The latter, a poorly endowed and overpopulated country, largely tribal in its attitudes towards land tenure, has not been able to afford the luxury of land reform and rehabilitation. Now independent, however, it is getting economic and technical help from its powerful neighbor, whose best interests will undoubtedly be served by offering it generously and quickly, particularly in the direction of conservation.

Among the many words of cautionary advice, those of the medical specialists are probably the most urgent. Until now, bilharzia (schistosomiasis) has been confined to east-flowing rivers, unable to cross the ecological barrier of the Escarpment, and to infect the highveld, except through low gaps made by the Pongola, Olifants, and Limpopo Rivers. Can bilharzia be kept away from the Orange Catchment? The medical experts, seeking prevention before cure, would give much to be able to hold the disease within its present bounds, but in Africa as elsewhere, irrigation has proved to be its best transportation agent.

Other Projects. Unfortunately, the Orange River Project has overshadowed many lesser water storage schemes which are nonetheless as important to South Africa's welfare. A second dam, below the existing Vaaldam, so vital to the southern Transvaal complex will be completed by 1970. The semiarid, once malaria-infected Makatini Flats of northern Zululand will by 1970 be irrigated from the Jozini Dam, holding back the waters of the Pongola River through a narrow gorge in the Lebombo Mountains, thus making available some 15,000 acres for sugar, rice, coffee, cotton, and other valuable cash crops. Combined desalination and power plants, based on nuclear heat-exchange plants, have already been proposed for a number of coastal areas, but these are incidental to the primary needs of a greater part of South Africa.

6 *Understanding South Africa*

THE RAPID emergence of South Africa as an industrial power, ranking high among the developing nations of the world, was a wholly unexpected phenomenon. It offered little chance of an equally rapid mental adjustment among the white communities, whose *raison d'etre* was rural isolation, independence, and republicanism. This has become even more obvious in new socioeconomic situations, where nonwhite groups were making their influence felt as industrial labor.

There is no need at this stage to present a detailed historical sketch of the country's evolution from a small supply garrison to a large, unified, and relatively sophisticated area. The period between 1652 and about 1865 would be recognizable as one of the expanding pioneer frontier, based on nomadic pastoralism over limitless unoccupied grasslands, adjusting itself to the undefined frontiers of Bantu nations by warfare or avoiding actions. It was an era during which several important attitudes in the Boer nation took deep root and evolved—pastoralism, religious fundamentalism, and republicanism. Slavery came and went, leaving behind a polygot community and colonial attitudes to manual labor which were probably responsible for the first racial discriminations.

GROWTH OF AFRIKAANS NATIONALISM

After diamonds and gold had been discovered on the highveld, there was set in motion a series of events whose repercussions resound in every corner of modern South Africa. The country became an important battleground for British imperialism in its most active and aggressive phase, culminating in the Anglo-Boer War of 1899–1902. The latter engendered mental attitudes which survive in certain Afrikaans communities as a virulent bitter hatred against their British "oppressors," whose massed armies only succeeded in reducing the Boer guerrilla forces to impotence by removing all women and children to concentration camps, where some 26,000 died, mainly from typhoid fever and other infections.

Forgiveness was difficult despite the generous peace terms of the British government, whose military power had been severely mauled during years of unconventional warfare. Without at least some understanding of the intensity of this period, the first nationalist struggle for self-determination in Africa, it is difficult to follow many of the political events of the twentieth century. The presence of a considerable English-speaking community, dominating commerce, industry, and the press, remained a thorn in the Boer flesh for another 50 years.

Yet, at the turn of the century, the Bantu nations offered no problem; they were stabilized in their reservations and abundantly supplied with land for cattle and cultivation, and warfare had ceased. Those Bantu in the Cape who had, in the same way as the Cape Coloureds, measured up to Cecil Rhodes' definition of a "civilized man" were enfranchised and had begun to seek national identity through vague political movements (pp. 151–52). Otherwise, they were a tribal subsistence people who did not enter into the economy. If there was a problem, it was mainly in Natal, where the Indian population was increasingly vocal and numerous.

Despite many mutual animosities, the four colonies, Transvaal, Cape, Orange Free State, and Natal, were persuaded to join a Union of South Africa which came into being in 1910. The Act of Union contained two "entrenched" clauses which protected the existing franchise rights of non-whites in the Cape Colony, and secondly, preserved both English and Afrikaans as equal, official languages. Without these guarantees, closer union would never have been effected.

Joining Great Britain in World War I, South African armed forces captured South-West Africa in a brilliant campaign, joined battle in German East Africa, and went on to Europe where they suffered heavy casualties. Though there were many Afrikaners in the armed forces, large numbers of *bitter-einders* (last ditchers) attempted a rebellion in 1914 in an attempt to gain independence.

THE ECLIPSE OF SMUTS

Fluctuating influences between 1920 and the outbreak of World War II made it obvious that unity between the two white groups was a far-distant prospect. The 1922 Witwatersrand rebellion and strike, fomented in part by Trotskyite elements in order to gain control of the labor force in the gold mines, was ruthlessly suppressed by General Smuts, the Prime Minister of the day, using troops, tanks, and artillery. In addition to crippling an important trade-union structure, this strike and its aftermath made Smuts unpopular among his fellow Afrikaners, who could not forgive him his predilection for the English. Leading the South African Party (later the United Party) at the polls, he relied on the entire English-speaking community and a section of the Afrikaners throughout the next quarter century, with the exception of a period of coalition government composed of the Nationalist and Labor parties between 1924 and 1929. It is possible that Smuts' methods of divide and rule delayed internal *entente* between the two white groups.

Anti-British Activities. Throughout the period from 1924 to 1948, political platforms were dominated by demands for a separate flag to replace the Union Jack, a new national anthem to replace "God Save the King," and a number of empty threats by Natal, the most "English" of the provinces, to secede from the Union in retaliation for these attacks on the British connection. These years prior to World War II were pervaded with powerful Nazi propaganda, aimed at restoring South-West Africa to Germany. Many agents working from South-West Africa itself encouraged the dissident Afrikaans groups in anti-British activities, which went as far as the formation of quasi-secret societies, as well as youth and Grey Shirt movements. Antisemitism, never before prominent in a country with so many Jewish communities, was added to the virulent hatreds in circulation. It would be unwise, however, to classify these Afrikaners (who have since become prominent in public affairs) as Nazi. They were expressing a strong anti-British feeling, which was exacerbated by Smuts' decision, based on a very slight parliamentary victory, to declare war on Germany and Italy in 1939 instead of remaining benevolently neutral.

Three years of sabotage, explosion, and subversion were ended once again by drastic action on the part of Smuts, who, by interning many Afrikaans men and women, paid the full price in the crucial 1948 general election. In his own electoral district he was ignominiously defeated by an ex-internee, and his United Party lost its long tenure as the ruling government to an unready Nationalist Party, somewhat surprised by its unexpected victory.

Having already suffered a serious blow at the United Nations General Assembly in 1946 on the question of South-West Africa, Smuts, one of the architects of that organization as well as of its predecessor, the League of Nations, faded from the contemporary domestic scene in South Africa. He had long since sealed the fate of the United Party, which had not been allowed to develop men with powerful enough personalities to succeed him as leader. As an opposition party, it has continued to lose momentum and parliamentary seats, surviving as a fossilized representative of the post-Union era, unable to supply the electorate with an alternative to the present National Government.

THE NATIONALIST GOVERNMENT

After their frustrating spell in the political wilderness, the victorious Nationalist Party (soon to be renamed the National Party) set about winning the last battles of the Anglo-Boer War in order to achieve the aims of their Voortrekker forefathers. Little thought was spared for those English-speaking South Africans who felt they still had a link with England, beyond the decision that the entrenched language clause in the Act of Union should be retained. In this campaign they had the support of two generations of Afrikaners instructed in the injustices of the Anglo-Boer War. They were reminded everywhere by monuments to the innocent victims; by patriotic poetry, much of it excellent; by the continued survival of the rebel heroes in their midst; and by the enshrinement of the Voortrekker folk myth.

Cultural Domination. The Afrikaans language, diverging from Nederlands-Dutch in the early nineteenth century, had become the vital core of a struggle for cultural identity which evoked the spirit of the family, the purity of rural farming communities, folk dancing, traditional games played with ox-yokes, and many other elements of the Golden Age. Afrikaans newspapers, journals, and novels, unilingual universities, and teacher-training colleges imbued the post-Boer War generations with a spirit of nationalism which, no matter how paltry and chauvinistic it may have appeared to contemporary observers, rose to a high flood.

In the background, the Calvinist Dutch Reformed Church pursued similar policies through its hold on the devout rural communities, strongly fundamentalist in their beliefs and relying on God to grant them their rightful place in the sun. Throughout the country, Nationalist-inspired banks, insurance, manufacturing, and cooperative enterprises gradually brought about an important economic exclusion of any organization or person without party affiliations. In this they were assisted by a secret society known as Die Broederbond (The Brotherhood), consisting of some 2,000 influential Afrikaners, whose main function was to ensure the dominance of the Afrikaans nation.

Racial Legislation. From traditionally weighted rural electoral districts the Nationalist Party derived the political strength to enact the many laws of racial discrimination which litter the South African landscape. Most of the racial legislation during the first six years of the National Government was deliberately negative. It pandered to the rural communities who saw in the rapid advancement of the Bantu in industry a threat to their supply of cheap farm labor and to the many thousands of "poor whites" whose very survival was threatened by Bantu competition. It appeased the conscience of a people whose forebears had helped to procreate the Cape Coloured people and Bantu Mulattos, (see page 45) by enacting laws forbidding sexual intercourse or marriage between different "racial" groups. It sanctified "racial purity" by identifying the shadowy boundaries between the four ethnic groups—Whites, Bantu, Asiatics and Coloured—no easy task for a government aware of its own supporters' genetic anomalies. As a result, *everybody* is now compelled to carry an identity card. Thus was social custom rigidified into Draconian law.

The most controversial legislation, however, was directed against the Cape Coloured peoples, whose peculiar privilege it had been in the liberal days of the Cape Colony to be enfranchised (together with a small number of Bantu) and to be protected from disenfranchisement by one of the two entrenched clauses in the Act of Union. Their concentration in the southwestern Cape Province and their liberal political attachments, together with the rate of natural increase, posed a threat to the predominantly Nationalist farmers of the region. Since an entrenched clause could be revoked only by a two-thirds majority of a joint sitting of the lower House of Assembly and the Senate, there ensued between 1950 and 1956 a long struggle in the political arena and in the law courts before the clause was invalidated and Cape Coloureds excluded even nominally from helping to administer their country.

Such indignities actually offended many of the government's supporters, since the Cape Coloureds had important status in many Afrikaans homes as family servants and general factotums. They were free to move in Cape Town society without hindrance and had made valuable contributions in the cultural-artistic world of dancing, opera, drama, and poetry. They had the reputation of being ambitious, industrious, pious, and members of the total community. Nonetheless, political pressures forced a not entirely willing government into this act of excision in order to save its southwestern white constituents from demographic annihilation.

Shift to the Highveld. Choosing a successor for Prime Minister Malan when he retired in 1954 exposed for the first time in public the rivalry between the Cape section and the combined Transvaal and Orange Free State segments of the monolithic National Party. The latter, composed of aggressive northerners with the consequences of rapid industrialization and urbanization, particularly of the Bantu, on their hands, asserted their authority over the comparatively liberal Cape element by electing their candidate Strijdom to the premiership.

Voortrekker philosophies, embodying among others *baasskap* (white supremacy) and the inferior role of Bantu and Coloureds as "hewers of wood and drawers of water," found their maximum expression from the outset. Many of Strijdom's public utterances have returned to haunt the government years after it had changed its stance and its outlook towards *apartheid* and had evolved its policy of *separate development,* now in action throughout the country. Much of this period was directed towards controlling the influx of rural Bantu into the towns and the fatuous attempts to persuade the white population that it should make itself completely independent of the Bantu in its domestic, industrial, and rural activities. At the same time, municipalities and central government alike were engaged in building large separate townships to replace the ghastly slums in the cities.

The Tomlinson Commission and Its Consequences. In 1955, the Tomlinson Commission (Commission for the Socio-Economic Development of the Bantu Areas Within the Union of South Africa) submitted its findings in thirteen large volumes of evidence to the House of Assembly. The cold facts of the parlous state of the Native Reserves, the socioeconomic effects of migratory labor on the Bantu communities, and most of all, their projected population growth from 10 million in 1955 to about 36 million by 2000, were carefully analyzed. Numerous suggestions were submitted to the government, including the idea of Bantu homelands, based on ethnolinguistic considerations.

The Commission estimated that about 290 million dollars would have to be provided during the next ten years in order to carry out the plans. Few documents could have had so powerful an effect on what, up to that moment, had been a complacent all-white legislature, content to ignore the realities. After debating its contents in 1956, the government repudiated the Commission's report in a

White Paper. Yet such are the uncertainties of the body politic that by 1959 the Promotion of Bantu Self-Government Act had been passed, opening the way for the creation of Bantu homelands, and by 1961 some $160 million had been set aside for a five-year development program. By 1963 the Transkei, a large consolidated area, had received its own legislature, had conducted a rational, general election, and had created a cabinet government of seven Bantu ministers of state and an opposition party (pages 158–159).

Changes in Policy. The profound changes in the National Party may safely be attributed to the powerful personality of Strijdom's successor, Dr. Hendrik Verwoerd, whose premiership ended in assassination in 1966. His rigid, unyielding determination to carry through a policy of separate development, not only of the Bantu but of the other three groups as well, earned him world opprobrium and in 1961 virtual expulsion from the British Commonwealth, of which South Africa had been an early and leading independent member for many years.

For Dr. Verwoerd and his National Party, nothing could have been more timely. Within months, after a closely contested referendum, the country became a republic and a troublesome umbilical cord had been severed. Many English-speaking citizens were initially distressed by this loss of association with the United Kingdom and the Commonwealth, while others were deeply concerned with a possible loss of trade advantages. That the transition occurred without major economic upsets was merely a reflection of the country's stability, particularly as a supplier of primary raw materials.

More surprising, however, were the inroads which Verwoerd was able to make into the English-speaking strongholds of Natal, Transvaal, and the Cape, not only electorally but also in terms of general acceptance of his philosophies of separate development as opposed to the beguiling never-never land of *baasskap*. Clearly, the loss of commonwealth status had been replaced by a growing loyalty to a South Africa, whose white populations were at last finding common ground. Nowhere has this idea of separate development found readier acquiescence than among the Indians of Natal, the vast majority of whom have had little difficulty in adjusting themselves to a "group area" in greater Durban and in developing socioeconomic class structures within their casteless society.

Fresh Approaches to Neighbors. Another of Verwoerd's minor triumphs was the outcome of his approach to the three protectorates of Basutoland (Lesotho), Bechuanaland (Botswana), and Swaziland as they came nearer to an independence which might have been mutually embarrassing. Three days before he was killed in the House of Assembly, Verwoerd had met Mr. Jonathon, Premier of Lesotho, in Cape Town, in order to raise a number of important economic matters. His successor, Dr. John Vorster, is proving even more flexible in his approach to these immediate African problems and has initiated a number of important diplomatic moves towards at least an economic *rapprochement* with countries even further afield. These include an exchange of ambassadors and a trade agreement with Malawi; provision of geological surveyors, technical advice, and facilities for training nurses to several independent African countries; and extensive sales of processed foods and machinery on a continental scale.

Facing Nationalist Policies. What emerges from the past ten years, and what is the Afrikaans political outlook? It is often assumed by commentators that this has remained static. True, the National Government has not altered its negative attitude towards social integration and universal franchise, but there is clearly an acceptance of economic and political changes within the framework of the policy of separate development which would have been impossible in the restrictive atmosphere of the 1948 electoral triumph. Attempts by a small right-wing splinter party in the 1966 general election to turn back the clock to *baasskap* were a disastrous failure, while extensive gains from the opposition United Party demonstrated the further acceptance of government policies among increasing numbers of the white population.

Freedom for the Bantu to purchase all kinds of alcoholic liquors was the result of a report submitted by a high-powered commission in 1961, which led to the very quick passage of an act through both Houses of Parliament, despite strong objections from the temperance lobby. Predicted murder, rapine, and looting failed to materialize on August 15, 1962, when the act became law or in the days and years following. The motivation for this action was not wholly altruistic, of course, and while the evils of Chicago-like gang warfare, smuggling, and crime accompanying illegal sales were reduced to insignificant proportions, the Cape wine growers benefited economically. What is more important, however, is the change of attitude.

Labor Requirements in Industry. Work Reservation, a process reserving certain skilled crafts to white hands, has been so shot through with amendments, under pressure of increasing shortages of skilled white labor, as to be almost irrelevant. Nowhere is it more surprising to see employment barriers dropped than in the postal services, in railway workshops, and other areas of powerful Afrikaans conservatism. Most private trucks are now driven by nonwhites who have been allowed to do so because it was agreed that each shall receive the same wage as a white man. Only in situations where poor whites have to be protected from Bantu workers is the policy strictly followed. This is common sense rather than logic, but for the politician the reality of these marginal overlaps has to be faced.

The Dutch Reformed Church in 1965 and 1966 published a resounding attack on the system of migratory labor used in mining and some industry, on the grounds that it destroys family life and the community. This bold stand, defying a fundamental principle of classical Boer theology, arises from several years of active eruption within the church administration following the Evanston Conference. Although church doctrine has not been as pro-*apartheid* as many of its critics think, its lay membership provides the National party's support. It is a measure of the intellectual metamorphosis which the theologians have experienced that they can argue their case in public.

Increasing movements of rural white Afrikaners to the towns, corresponding loss of a sense of isolation, and increased educational facilities have all changed the Afrikaans' attitude, especially when they are thrown more closely into contact with the northern industrial Bantu worker. There is today a slowly increasing mutual respect which originates in the need to improve productivity, and great educational strides have been made on the factory floor in training white supervisors of Bantu labor to appreciate cultural and social peculiarities. Only in the field of mining has there been any reluctance on the part of Nationalist dominated white unions to allow the Bantu worker to possess the vital document—the blasting certificate—a major barrier to advancement for the Bantu who work underground.

The Triumphs of Afrikanerdom. Most significant of the influences playing upon the mind of the Afrikaans nation is the actual experience it has undergone since 1948. Until then, it had looked back, not without some masochistic pleasure, over fifty years of oppression, able to blame upon the British, Botha, Smuts, and even Hertzog, all the ills of farming life, including drought, flood, and locusts. In 1948, the year of Nationalist triumph, began a long season of wrongs (both real and imagined) being put to right, culminating in the self-respect of a Republic.

After March 1961 there were no more battles to be fought against the traditional folk-enemy, the British government. The Afrikaner today is so relaxed that his mentors now worry about his failure to keep Afrikaans a "pure" language, to maintain the traditional ways of Afrikanerdom, and to remain a devout member of the Dutch Reformed Church. He is now to be found in business, industry, technology, often as a senior executive, able to hold his own in what was once an exclusively English-speaking domain. From this vantage point, he recognizes problems which must be discussed and not turned aside. The gradual shift in balance of power from country to the town reinforces this trend. The need to export manufactured goods and primary materials requires an outward-facing attitude. Aggressive salesmanship in Latin America, a growing merchant marine, a large sugar-cane mill built for Malawi, are but a few of the elementary signs of the decline of the "White-Laager" mentality (isolationism) in which he once took refuge from the outside world.

BANTU NATIONALISM

Subsistence Life in the Reserves. Once they were conquered by force of arms, the Bantu peoples without exception committed themselves to the care and protection of successive colonial governments in the Cape and Natal during the nineteenth century. By doing so they avoided mass genocide, the common fate elsewhere of most primitive peoples who resisted the white man's aggression. They were allocated specific areas, known as Native Reserves, in which tribal law and traditions were allowed to hold sway without interference from their colonial masters. For many tribes, this was the heyday of their existence. Land was plentiful, the pastures rich, and Pax Britannica ensured their survival by preventing the resurgence of internecine wars and by reducing the risks of starvation and pestilence. Under such circumstances, some of the finest well-watered lands of South Africa came under Bantu control, only to be slowly ravaged during the twentieth century by overpopulation, overstocking, misuse, and soil erosion.

Economic activities among the white communities of South Africa impinged only slightly upon the subsistence Reserve life in its early years. Despite a slowly emerging pattern of squatter- and sharecropping tenancy on white farms in the latter half of the nineteenth century, the tribal economy persisted. Few cattle left the Reserves, and surpluses of food crops were absorbed locally mainly in the form of seasonal beer parties. Both before and after their subjugation, the Zulu nation contemptuously dismissed employment in the Natal sugarcane fields as "women's work." The result was the introduction of East Indian indentured labor. Similarly, Bantu reluctance to work in the Witwatersrand gold mines led to the importation of Chinese laborers in 1904. Yet both situations were soon reversed when it became necessary for the Bantu to find money to pay hut and poll taxes.

Bantu males began increasingly to migrate from their Reserves to the economic centers of the country as temporary sojourners, thus providing the means to survive rising agrarian pressures without the need to reform the systems of tribal land tenure, to cull the growing herds of livestock, or to intensify methods of cultivation. The result is written upon the face of most Reserves today, for in spite of missionary and government efforts to effect changes, little of lasting value was accomplished against the traditional conservatives, who attributed their parlous situation to the government's refusal to grant increased land areas for their extended use.

Bantu Urbanization. With large-scale industrialization, migratory labor among Bantu men (and eventually among women) increased rapidly until the demographic imbalance not only reduced all the reserves to economic impotence but also persuaded many thousands not to return from the city to their poverty-stricken homes. World War II accelerated this process of urbanization which was immediately recognizable in the many shanty towns and slums with their overcrowding, crimes, and diseases so effectively described by Alan Paton in his romantic novel *Cry the Beloved Country.*

TABLE 17
Bantu Urbanization
(in thousands)

Year	*Total*	*Urban*	*Rural*
1904	3,490	361	3,129
1911	4,019	524	3,495
1921	4,697	658	4,039
1936	6,596	1,252	5,344
1946	7,831	1,902	5,928
1951	8,560	2,391	6,169
1960	10,928	3,471	7,457

Source: Statistical Year Book 1965.

Rural depopulation and accelerated drift to the towns (Table 17) is now a familiar worldwide problem, but South African cities were more fortunate than most in being able to absorb these immigrants in rapidly expanding mining, industrial, and commercial sectors of the national economy. By 1945, in fact, some 65% of the country's industrial work force was Bantu, mainly engaged in unskilled and semiskilled labor. Few of them, however, were adequtely housed.

Coping with the Drift to Town. In order to eliminate all shanty towns and slum conditions, both city and government administrations have been engaged since 1950 in vast low-cost housebuilding programs, creating new towns, transport facilities, and other amenities such as clinics, schools, and shopping centers, all of which meet the requirements of the *apartheid* or separate development which is the present government's political philosophy. Repugnant though it may be to the outside world, this doctrinal approach to a socioeconomic problem has brought about a successful housing revolution more rapidly than would otherwise have been possible. It has probably eliminated the city slum in South Africa for several generations to come, because provision has been made for future expanding populations as well as the present one.

Economic Stimulation of the Bantu Reserves. For many observers, however, the economic problems of Bantu development are concentrated in the Reserves, where productivity is too slow to support those who *must* come off the land if it is to be used efficiently. Political decisions have been made by the National Government to reduce the flow of city-bound Bantu immigrants to a rate which is roughly equal to the number of jobs available, thus making it more urgent to examine the dilemma of the Reserves in the light of projected population growth. The Tomlinson Commission, reporting in 1955, indicated a number of ways in which it might be possible to develop these areas so that they could play their part in the South African economy. Once again these plans have become closely linked with government policies aimed at the development of the Bantu nations in their so-called homelands, their ethnic tribal areas, and represent the outcome of more than a century's struggle between various groups for political domination.

Evolution of Land Policies for the Bantu. Land rights and the franchise for all non-whites in South Africa, and particularly for the Bantu, have long been the cornerstone of liberal political parties in the white community. The Cape Colony view of common citizenship for all, established as early as 1852, was embodied in the constitution of 1872 granting responsible government to the Cape Colony. A property and income qualification was therefore the only limit to franchise for the Cape Coloured, Bantu, and White alike. In Natal, however, a similar liberal outlook lasted only nine years after the charter of Natal in 1856. In the Orange Free State, where the problem could hardly be said to exist, the 1854 Bloemfontein Convention made it quite clear that all but Whites were excluded from the franchise.

Most definite of all, however, was the Transvaal Republic's constitution of 1858 (*Grondwet*), Clause 9 of which stated "The people desire to permit no equality between Coloured people and the white inhabitants, either in Church or State." This categorical declaration, known later as "the northern principle" had been formulated in Potchefstroom in 1844 soon after the Great Trek had accomplished its purpose and the Boers had left behind them the Hottentot thieves, freed slaves, and other non-Whites who had made their lives so miserable. The Trekker leaders had no intention, therefore, of allowing their rural utopian republics to be overrun by similar persons, and preserved such negativistic policies throughout the nineteenth and early twentieth centuries in their constitutions, even after their defeat in the Anglo-Boer War.

The Northern Principle. Throughout the period of the National Convention, which had been charged with the preparation of the Act of Union of the four colonies, the contrasted northern and southern principles of race relations was a constant source of friction between its members. The British government, anxious only to restore its battered prestige after the Boer War, made few attempts to represent the views of the non-white populations, themselves standing helplessly on the sidelines. An entrenched clause preserved the more liberal Cape Colony from losing its Cape Coloured and Bantu franchise, but elsewhere the general attitude among the delegates was restrictive, and as the "northern principle" became dominant in national policy in the years following, even the Cape remnants vanished.

The history of land policy in South Africa with regard to the Bantu is complex. A flurry of proclamations in the last decade of the nineteenth century formalized not only the Native Reserve boundaries but also those of the Protectorates. The Glen Grey Act of 1894 laid the foundation for self-government in the Transkei. The South African Native Affairs Commission, which reported in 1905, established the basis for all official policy in the half century following, principally on the subject of the exclusion of Bantu from freehold rights to land in "white" areas. There were many other commissions, parliamentary bills, and acts which sought to define policy towards squatting, territorial segregation, and the attrition of land and franchise rights preserved by the Bantu in the Cape. Among these were the Native Lands Act (1913), the Native Affairs Administration Bill of 1917, and among others, the most important of all, the Native Trust and Land Act and the Representation of Natives in Parliament Act of 1936. Not all the legislation enacted was repressive. In 1936, for example, the decision to purchase 15.34 million acres of white lands contiguous to existing Reserves (22.71 million acres) was a bold and politically dangerous step which has been carried through steadily to the present day. On the other hand, the Cape Bantu franchise was removed in the same year and representation of all Bantu embodied in four elected white senators, three white members of the lower House of Assembly, and a Native Representative Council, partly elected and partly nominated. The latter was adjourned *sine die* in 1947 after an undistinguished career. White representation for the Bantu in both houses persisted until it was eliminated in 1961.

While most attention was diverted towards the Reserves and rural areas, it was clear in the post-World War II years that great changes had taken place in the distribution of Bantu peoples. Urbanization had crept up on Parliament and the administration almost unobserved. Hence the Report of the Native Laws Commission, 1946–48, known as the Fagan Report, was a brilliant review of the effects of the African Pass Laws, migratory labor, and certain types of urban legislation on urban and rural Bantu. Unfortunately, this was published during the critical period of changeover from United Party to Nationalist Party government so that many of the liberalizing recommendations were ignored. The decade which followed upon the Nationalist Party victory was rather one of increasingly restrictive legislation, designed for the most part to meet the prejudices of a rural white electorate long indoctrinated for this moment of sweet triumph.

Separate Development. Among the South African electorate, the new word, *apartheid,* was used to describe a number of situations, most of which implied "the ultimate goal of a natural process of separate development" and which were applicable not only to Bantu and White but also to East Indians and Cape Coloureds, each of which was expected to develop into a self-sufficient unit. The vicissitudes of this dogma have been recorded in many places—through protest marches, passive resistance, parliamentary debate, the formation of new parties, sabotage, and most of all, through the implications of the Commission for the Socio-Economic Development of the Bantu Areas Within the Union of South Africa (better known as the Tomlinson Commission). The latter provided a blueprint for carrying in part to its logical conclusion the "northern principle" of total separation.

Against every expressed wish of the outside world, the various ethnic communities of South Africa have been taken along the road to total separation from one another in all but industry and commerce. All towns have been made subject to a Group Areas Act, which divides urban areas into four ethnic zones, with a common industrial and business zone. Since only a few towns have in fact been able to finalize their plans, this is more a long-term program which will only gradually disentangle the ethnic knot.

The most important legislation introduced after the Tomlinson Report was, however, the Promotion of Bantu Self-Government Act, which became law in 1959. In the first place, it removed the white senators and M.P.'s representing non-white interests from their seats. Secondly, it brought into being the idea of several "nations" among the Bantu peoples, whose existence was to be recognized through a territorial authority and a commissioner general, each in a "homeland" whose advancement to self-government would be attained through constitutional evolution. It was considered that urban members of each "nation" would have the right to vote in their respective homeland, thus evading the problem of national constitutional rights for the urbanized Bantu. Lest it be thought that these were vague, undetermined proposals, it should be realized that five territorial authorities now exist and a sixth has acquired a degree of independence which has enabled it to carry out an election based on literate universal franchise, to form a cabinet, and to develop a two-party system. Here, then, is the ultimate aim of political separation.

The Growth of Bantu Political Parties. In order to oppose earlier land policies, there were early attempts to unite Bantu opinion in the Cape Province. The Native Education Association, formed in 1882 to protest the British Colonial Pass Laws, was succeeded in 1884 by the Native Electoral Association with the avowed purpose of encouraging enfranchised Cape Bantu to use their electoral rights. Despite the existence of a Natal and a Transvaal Native Congress after the Anglo-Boer War, there was little evidence of an emergent Bantu nationalistic spirit to counter the virility of Afrikaner nationalism until the Union Convention began its deliberations in 1908. By this time a number of Bantu men who had attended British and American universities, after graduating from several highly reputed local mission colleges, had become the articulate spokesmen for their peoples. The failure of the Native Convention, sent to the United Kingdom to seek direct representation for the Bantu in the Act of Union, led to the formation of the South African Native National Congress in 1912 under the presidency of Dr. John L. Dube. This body, later known as the African National Congress (A.N.C.) became the political focus for African leaders, attacking the pass laws and various land acts involving the Bantu.

While similar organizations provided the nucleus for many future governments elsewhere in Africa, this congress failed signally to accomplish its purpose in South Africa. With a multiracial community in mind, the African National Congress pursued for many years a policy of nonviolent activity, seeking alliances with the South African Indian Congress, the White Congress of Democrats (later to become fronts for Marxist activism), and the various Cape Coloured Organizations. Tribal rivalries and the formation of dissident groups such as the Industrial and Commercial Union (I.C.U.) under a Nyaslander, Clemens Kadalie, in the 1920's prevented any show of unity. At the same time, trade unionism seldom proved to be a rallying point, mainly because most Bantu labor at the time was migratory.

Communist Influences. From 1946 onwards, all Bantu and Indian political movements, including the African National Congress, were infiltrated with varying degrees of success by well-trained Marxist cadres which since 1922 had been preparing for the take-over of the only truly industrial proletariat in Africa. Repressive government legislation, including the Suppression of Communism Act of 1950, was increasingly resisted by all non-White "liberal" movements in the country, using stay-at-home strikes, bus boycotts, passive resistance campaigns—all with scant success. Under the leadership of Robert Sobukwe, a young Zulu scholar, the Pan-African Congress (P.A.C.), a breakaway movement of the A.N.C., was formed, with an avowed policy of Bantu domination of South Africa. Sobukwe, following the techniques of countries further to the north, boasted in 1959 that he would take over the reins of government in 1963 with his hand-picked cabinet. His group's policy was designed to appeal not only to the intellectuals but also to the rural peasantry and illiterates, ultimately through violence, sabotage, and guerrilla warfare, financed in part from Chinese-Communist sources. Both organizations were banned in 1960.

Terrorist Tactics. The ensuing years between 1960 and 1964 proved to be the testing period for both A.N.C. and P.A.C. strength. Their leaders were banned from taking any part in political life, imprisoned, or forced to flee the country, after protracted harassment by government, police, and security forces. During this period, they alienated most of their Bantu and Indian supporters, who shied away from violent Mau-Mau-like tactics of terrorization and from proven connections with Chinese Communist activities.

Some hundreds of young Bantu men have, however, traveled secretly northward since 1964, first to Algerian base camps, then through Cairo and Pakistan to Chinese guerrilla training areas to form the nucleus of a future force to be directed from Dar es Salaam, Zanzibar, and other anti-*apartheid* centers. Several hundred of them, armed with Czech and Chinese guns, were present in 1967 in areas north of South-West Africa, trying to terrorize the Ovambo and others into submission—with little success. Another group attempting to infiltrate from Zambia through Rhodesia was badly mauled in Wankie Game Reserve in August 1967 by Rhodesian and South African security forces. Anti-terrorist legislation was enacted to cope with this kind of activity, and severe warnings conveyed to the Zambian government about the risks involved. On the other hand, internal bases such as Lesotho and Botswana became less sympathetic to the cause in the later 1960's, and faced by an excellent intelligence service within and beyond the Republic's borders, no group has been able so far to infiltrate the country in any strength.

Pan Africanism. Regardless of personal feelings in this matter, it should be recognized that the Pan-African ideal seems unlikely to run the same course in South Africa as it has in the rest of Negro Africa. The Bantu homelands on the one hand offer the politically ambitious the chance to advance themselves within their tribal areas; on the other hand, the present generation of economically ambitious townsmen are anxious only to maintain a peaceful, stable milieu in which to improve their lot and emulate the white man. Furthermore, much of the malevolent and bitter distrust of the "white oppressor" has been dissipated by the latter's almost impeccable attitudes towards the Bantu people since 1963. Promises have been kept and intentions quickly translated into reality. African police have displaced white in most Bantu urban and rural areas; 1,600 Education Committees, composed entirely of local Bantu men and women, supervise their own schools; excellent radio news services and widely read newspapers in all languages offer abundant evidence of the consequences of violence elsewhere in Africa and Asia.

The Pan-African Congress and the African National Congress can therefore offer little beyond the classical blood, sweat and tears to people who, despite deep resentments of such things as inadequate transport for the journey to work, are unlikely to respond to the clarion call to man the barricades for some time to come. By the time they are ready to do so, much will have changed not only in the Republic of South Africa itself, but in the rest of the African continent.

7 Separate Development in Action

After Premier Verwoerd had in 1959 outlined his policy for developing the Bantu homelands, many observers dismissed it as a wholly impractical dream, in view of the large sums required to rehabilitate the Reserves, to speed up education and technical training, and to stimulate their economic development. They regarded it as a mere party political maneuver to placate a restive white electorate. Others looked upon the diversion of energy from the main industrial centers as an economic heresy, pointing out what the Tomlinson Report had already indicated: that Bantu urban populations in the "white" cities would still total 11,000,000 by the year 2000 even if the current flow from the country to the town could be reversed in the near future.

A set of unforeseen circumstances, however, changed patterns of government thinking very quickly. Departure from the Commonwealth, republican status, and the distressing, needless Sharpeville incident involving the killing of some sixty Bantu during a township protest against the pass laws were all salutory shocks. The discrediting of many of the non-white leaders, after it had been conclusively shown that they were avowed Marxists, increased international attacks upon *apartheid,* and Verwoerd's personal determination all helped to set in motion a program of deliberate, continuing development of the homelands in concert with a number of associated carefully planned projects.

BANTU HOMELANDS

Regardless of his personal value judgments, the reader should grasp this essential point. A vast socioeconomic plan on a scale akin to many in such socialist countries as the Soviet Union, with an avowed aim of "separate development," was set in motion in 1961. Its ramifications are now so extensive and all-embracing that nothing except a violent revolution or war is likely to alter its general course. Details will undoubtedly be altered to meet changing conditions, and even though separate development may in the long run be abandoned in favor of social and economic integration, the plan as it applies to the Native Reserves in South Africa and South-West Africa is likely to proceed without serious opposition from white and non-white alike.

The progress or otherwise of this plan will be examined with interest by all students of planning techniques in developing countries, for the problems of the South African Native Reserves are microcosmic samples of problems that beset most sub-Saharan countries. Persisting tribal nationalisms which refuse to bury their differences are proving themselves to be the major barrier to the unification of many African countries. Nigeria, Sierra Leone, and Ghana, for example, have recently been forced to accept tribal separateness or face continual civil war for another generation. Has South Africa stumbled upon a workable alternative solution for that vital intermediate period between tribalism and fully integrated society?

The Former Protectorates (British High Commission Territories). Of course, the Bantu homeland idea envisaged more than just the rehabilitation of the Bantu Reserves within the Republic. The British Protectorates of Bechuanaland, Basutoland, and Swaziland were viewed by the Tomlinson Commission as part of the architectural scheme, embodying as they did largely homogeneous Bantu nations suffering precisely the same problems as their rural neighbors. Once granted their political independence by Great Britain, Bechuanaland (Botswana) and Basutoland (Lesotho)—both landlocked, poverty-stricken territories—have moved rapidly towards an economic *entente* with South Africa, despite its racially directed political system. Having abandoned the vague premise in the Act of Union that the protectorates should eventually be absorbed, South Africa has been able to accept all three as Bantu "nations." Their independent existence offers few threats to her security beyond their possible limited use as bases for Chinese-Communist-inspired conspirators, who now threaten the assassination of those in each territory who cooperate with South Africa.

Ox Bow Scheme. The appointment of a four-man commission to examine the feasibility of the Ox Bow Water scheme (page 128), of a prominent South African captain of industry at $1.00 per year to advise on the economic development of Lesotho, together with open invitations to South African industrialists to invest in Botswana's rich mineral resources were the first steps. Recent amicable discussions concerning Custom Union fees and migrant labor regulations and close liaison existing already between the King of Swaziland and the Republic, merely reinforce the already powerful trading links between the ex-protectorates and their neighbor. A problem once regarded by most authorities as insoluble because it was considered to be a territorial one, appears to have succumbed to mutual economic self-interest. As Robert Gardiner, executive secretary of the Economic Commission for Africa, remarked recently, "These territories are not hostages of South Africa!"

South-West Africa. Now that South-West Africa is, to all intents and purposes, considered an integral part of the Republic, the homelands policy will also be applied there. The Odendaal Commission in 1964 gave detailed consideration to ways of granting internal self-government to the Ovambo, Herero, Bergdamara, and others. The Ovambo have been invited for example to consider quasi-independence by 1968 and the Okavango soon afterwards.

EVOLUTION OF THE BANTU HOMELANDS

The first step towards clearer identification and administration of eight ethnic groups—Xhosa, Zulu, Tswana, Venda, Swazi, Tsonga, North Sotho, and South Sotho—from the 264 fragmented rural areas allocated to Bantu, was the Bantu Authorities Act (1951), creating tribal, regional, and territorial authorities whose functions were to formalize what had been rather haphazard relations between tribal chiefs and the central government. By 1963, six Territorial Authorities had been proclaimed, each of which could, under the Bantu Self-Government, Act of 1959, seek a quasi-independent status, roughly equivalent to that which exists between the Commonwealth of Puerto Rico and the U.S.A. The period of transition to Bantu Authority government was not wholly satisfactory owing to tribal reluctance to accept much-needed administrative reforms, to deliberate attempts on the part of well-known Communists to foment disorder, and to the need to unscramble certain complex ethnically mixed areas. It is generally accepted today, however, as the first essential step towards self-government.

The Transkei. Fortunately for the central government, there was at hand a large territorial unit with a relatively long period of stability, known as the Transkei. This territory, after its annexation in 1894 by the Cape government, went through a series of legislative steps from tribal magistracies to general councils, culminating in the well-known "Bunga" or United Transkeian Territories General Council. In an attempt to bring more Bantu into administration, the Bunga was dissolved and replaced in 1958 by the Transkeian Territorial Authority, composed of a Bantu chairman and executive and 123 tribal and communal authorities.

By January 1962 this Territorial Authority had claimed from Premier Verwoerd the right to self-government, which was granted after a full year of constitutional discussions revolving mostly round the role of the tribal chiefs in a democratically elected chamber. The Transkei Constitution Act came into existence on May 24, 1963, and was followed by a general election, the establishment of a two-party debating chamber, and all the trappings of Westminster democracy. Cabinet responsibility was assigned to the Departments of Agriculture, Forestry, Education, Welfare and Labor, Transport, Finance, Interior, and Justice; while Defense, Foreign Affairs, and some aspects of Justice remained within the purview of the central government in Pretoria. All cabinet ministers have retained a white adviser-secretary until such time as a local Transkeian can replace him. There are already some 2,000 Transkeian civil servants out of a total of 2,500, and in recent months a number of towns which used to be exclusively white have been zoned solely for Bantu occupation and purchase.

The Economic Needs of the Transkei. While it was a relatively simple process to introduce a new constitution into the Transkei Territory, the task of bringing economic growth is much more difficult and protracted. Though not apparently favored with exploitable mineral wealth, the Transkei has good soils, considerable areas of cultivable land, and adequate rainfall. It has suffered from soil erosion, overstocking, and a growing population problem for at least 30 years. Planned "betterment" programs, originally introduced by the Bunga, proved to be valueless until the Territorial Authority was able to persuade its people democratically to accept land-use capability surveys, fencing, culling of livestock, contour ploughing, and commercial forestry on the watershed slopes.

Remarkable progress has been made throughout the area in relocation of villages, churches, and schools and planning of land use, while local grasses have demonstrated their ability to restore once-eroded pastures if properly managed under fenced rotation systems. Some 4,000 miles of barbed-wire fencing are now being erected every year. Small agricultural shows, stock sales, and local demonstrations have done much to introduce a cash-crop outlook among the farming communities. The central government has deliberately encouraged the Transkeian Department of Agriculture to cultivate tea, a labor-intensive crop, in the interests of self-sufficiency, and New Zealand flax (*Phormium tenax*) as a substitute for imported jute. Irrigation farming of cotton and a number of subtropical crops is being carefully reviewed.

None of these progressive steps, however, alters the fundamental problem—that of removing some 50% to 70% of the present rural population from the countryside in order to enlarge current landholdings to an economic size. A beef deboning factory, a furniture and prefabricated house factory, and a wool mill provide only comparatively slight industrial employment, although forestry is absorbing several thousand males. Some 230 of the 635 trading stores, owned by whites, have already been sold to the Xhosa Development Corporation, a subsidiary of the Industrial Development Corporation (page 127), for disposal to local Transkeians after they have been commercially trained. Several hundred businesses and commercial activities have also been underwritten by the Corporation, which, through savings banks, is persuading the local population to provide loan capital for further enterprises.

Premier Verwoerd was adamant from the outset that he would resist the direct entry of white capital and enterprises into the Transkei until the latter specifically requested it, pleading that he did not wish to be accused of neocolonialism by the next generation of Transkeians. With his passing, this rigid rule has been gradually relaxed in order to accelerate the pace of economic development, and in one way or another, white capital is now becoming a direct and vital part of the process.

The Transkei is the first homeland or Bantustan. It owes its origin to a bold, apparently foolhardy Verwoerd who wagered his political career on its successful transition from traditional tribalism to relative modernity. Its ministers are equally bold and have not so far had to compromise their consciences despite a heavy subvention from the central government. They have recently voted overwhelmingly against further steps to total independence until better prepared to carry it through.

The Transkei government supports "separate development" while the opposition bench under the guidance of Knowledge Guzana opts for a form of multiracialism. The territory has seldom been quieter or more orderly. Yet the nagging questions which face all economic development planners have still to be answered. Is the rate of economic growth too slow? Can these good-quality lands yield cash crops? Will it be possible to introduce a number of local industries? Can the building of towns and of the associated infrastructure associated with them provide the economic spark for continued growth?

Other Bantu Homelands. If the answers to these questions were *easily* available, it would be possible for the government to incubate other homelands, none of which, however, would have the Transkei's advantages. The Zululand Reserves are badly fragmented and occupy rough, dissected lands on the eastern flank of the country; and although large numbers of Bantu farmers cultivate sugar cane on the coastal lowlands, many of the Zulu nation would have to move into other areas, such as the irrigable flood plains of the Pongola River. On the other hand, prospects for industrial development are relatively greater, owing to the presence of the Natal coal fields and the Tugela River Basin, particularly since the choice of Richards' Bay as a growth point.

It is more than likely that Tswanaland will be the second homeland in the Republic. Although less well-placed climatically, this national unit is more homogeneous than any other and has gradually been evolving a cadre of civil servants and potential cabinet ministers which is now drafting a constitution entitling it to homeland independence.

Education and Technical Training. Much of the progress of the homelands will obviously depend on the educational system. Several schools for the education and training of the sons of tribal chiefs have been established in key areas in order to provide well-trained administrators, continuity of government, and modernization. There is a severe shortage of teachers everywhere, without any prospect of a crash program which might cope with educational needs in the next generation. The controversial yet successful tribal university colleges, located as close to the various homelands as possible, are proving more satisfactory in the training of undergraduates for a first degree than was ever considered possible.

It is however, in technical fields such as engineering, pharmacy, and the sciences that the lack of trained men is most evident. If the Bantu homelands are to function successfully within the accepted limits of "separate development," there must surely be effective Bantu substitutes for the white men who hold such technical posts. This is the dilemma of nearly all developing countries, where blue-collar jobs are not highly regarded. Degrees in psychology, history, politics, and literature are still regarded as the necessary adjuncts to success among non-white students in South Africa, whereas scholarships for engineering remain unfilled. For this reason alone a second five year plan, to cost some $870 million, for Bantu areas (excluding the Transkei and South-West Africa) has allocated no less than $230 million to education.

COLOURED AND INDIAN DEVELOPMENT

With all matters concerning Bantu welfare, education, and development (excluding the Transkei) unified in a single, central Department of Bantu Affairs, it was considered a logical step to treat the Cape Coloured and Indian communities in a similar manner, although they cannot be said to possess "homelands" like the Bantu nations. As well as defining certain residential and business zones in the urban areas for their exclusive use, the government set up a nominated Advisory Council for each group as a contact group with the Department of Coloured Affairs and the Department of Indian Affairs, respectively, until elected bodies come into being.

A Coloured Representative Council, with 10 nominated members and 30 others representing 18 constituencies in the Cape, 6 in the Transvaal and 3 each in Natal and the Orange Free State, was to be elected by all Coloured adults of 21 years and over at the end of 1968 or early 1969. This Council, with comprehensive legislative and administrative powers, was scheduled to take over in 1969 a greater part of the Department of Coloured Affairs. Elections for a preparatory all Coloured Management Committee were held on November 29, 1967. A Coloured Development Council has also been established to channel funds into promising areas of development.

The Indian community has also been placed under a Department of Indian Affairs, which has taken over most of the functions previously delegated to the Provinces. A National Indian Council under the chairmanship of the departmental secretary, consisting of 21 Indians representing various sections of this heterogeneous community, was established in 1964 in order to provide some contact with the government until such time as the Indians are "able to elect representatives on accepted democratic norms." Despite their turbulent role in South African political history, the Indians appear to have accepted this opportunity, in the hope that it will provide some amelioration of the Group Area Laws which have affected their trading position in the cities. An elected Indian Representative Council, which could absorb the functions of the Department of Indian Affairs, is likely to come sooner than anticipated, for there are already many highly qualified professional men and business leaders who would be ready to serve their community in a legislative capacity.

BORDER INDUSTRIAL REGIONS

The Bantu homelands have not been allowed to develop in total isolation. Considering that it would not be politic to introduce white capital into them, the central government evolved a policy of industrial development in areas as close to the homeland boundaries as possible. This offered a Bantu worker the opportunity to take up employment in a factory without having to travel to the large industrial centers as a migrant laborer, while living with his family in a freehold house on lands specifically reserved for Bantu occupation in the homeland. These areas are known as the Border Industrial Regions.

Decentralization. Such a policy was also considered desirable since it was to all intents and purposes one of decentralization of industry which would in time not only reverse the flow of Bantu labor to the town but also avoid many of the well-known world problems associated with continually expanding metropolitan areas. There is considerable evidence that the policy is already achieving its principal purposes.

Selecting the eight major Border Regions was, from 1957 onwards, the task of the Natural Resources Development Council in consultation with several other government agencies. Suitable areas with abundant water supplies and other industrial services had also to show considerable short-term potential for growth. Once the Permanent Committee for the Location of Industry and the Development of Border Industries was established in 1960, great attention was given to the type of industrial undertaking best suited to the Border Regions and the concessions required to attract investment.

Types of Industries. The council favored industries which were labor-intensive and would absorb large numbers of Bantu workers from their homeland. It offered income tax concessions (rather in the form of depreciation and investment allowances than in freedom from annual taxes) and financial assistance (through the Industrial Development Corporation) in the form of share capital or low interest loans. Basic service facilities such as water, electricity, and transport were guaranteed to all users, while many factory buildings were built to investors' specifications for lease and ultimate purchase. Extensive financial assistance was granted to white personnel wanting to build new homes. Investors could also assume that workers' wages in the Border Regions would remain lower than those of urban-industrial areas for some time to come—a natural outcome of lower living costs and lower productivity. At the same time the Department of Bantu Administration carried out a program of housebuilding and infrastructural work *within* the neighboring Bantu homeland in order to provide permanent homes for factory workers. As a result some 25,000 houses have been built in fifteen homeland townships since 1960.

Investment in the Border Regions. Between 1960 and 1966, about $450 million (including $115 million in basic services) have been invested in the Border Regions. Some 90 new undertakings were established and 60 more extended with State assistance while 50 new projects and extensions were set up without government aid. It is difficult to calculate the number of Bantu involved in these operations; figures vary between 50,000 and 110,000, depending upon the way industry and services are defined. The South African Industrial Corporation has invested nearly $50 million in the form of loans or share capital. Afrikaans financial institutions with vast insurance and cooperative surpluses to invest have recently begun to interest themselves in these Border Industries.

Since 1960, more attention has been devoted to Border Regions conveniently located near the larger cities but having nevertheless a Bantu homeland nearby for residential development. Thus the four major areas—Rosslyn some 14 miles north of Pretoria, Hammarsdale 20 miles inland from Durban, Mdantsane just outside East London, and Zwelitsha near Queenstown—have attracted the largest number of industries so far. A fifth area, Phalaborwa, associated mostly with the extraction of copper, magnetite, and phosphates in the northern Transvaal, has great growth potential and is likely to become a focus for lowveld agriculture and for other neighboring mineral areas such as Steelport, with its immense chrome ore deposits, and Waterberg, with its rich coalbeds. Another promising area centers on Rustenburg in the western Transvaal which produces platinum, tobacco, and citrus.

Such areas offer few obstacles to economic growth. As long as Bantu townships can be built, industrialists are prepared to risk their capital in exchange for the excellent amenities provided. They will themselves be near enough to cities not to feel any isolation. Sooner or later, the more remote Border areas will, however, have to be brought into the picture. Located at great distances from the markets, without first-class transport and certain other services, they will attract only a restricted group of industries, and these only after incentives and concessions have been increased. Of these areas, the Tugela River Basin is likely to be the most important, once new railroad lines and the new Zululand port have been constructed. The only hope of the Zulu nation, in fact, lies in the rapid growth of its adjacent Border Areas, which could remove its unwanted rural population, enabling it to adopt a rational, planned agricultural program.

Textile manufacturing is probably the most important industry in the wide range of Border Industries. Very large mills have been established at East London, Zwelitsha, and Hammarsdale. In 1962 the government, recognizing the absence of at least 15 categories of textiles in the country, allocated some $63 million over a ten-year period to encourage their development. Food processing, timber conversion, high quality "instant" houses of timber and aluminum, concrete products, button manufacture, paper, cellulose and pulp manufacture, mineral extraction, shoes, and hosiery are but a few of the activities in these areas. With the opening of a large Japanese motor vehicle assembly plant at Rosslyn, near Pretoria, a pattern has been set for French, Italian, and American automobile companies to enter and develop this particular industry in the Border Regions. Bantu men, technically trained from scratch for the assembly line, have proved most successful competitive and productive workers who, in the Japanese company's collective eye, will soon be potential buyers of its product in large quantities. Six miles away—in fact, within the boundary of the Western Sotho Territorial Authority—lies Ga-Rankuwa, a new town of 4,000 houses from which the Rosslyn workers commute daily by train, bus, and bicycle.

Other Applications. In view of the great stress laid on decentralization of industry, it has proved possible for the Border program to be applied elsewhere than in the Bantu homelands. In depressed areas where unemployment among Cape Coloureds or Indians is high, the Permanent Committee has granted similar privileges to white and Indian industrialists for setting up new industries. A textile mill producing very high-quality poplin has, for example, been set up by Indian industrialists near Tongaat, a small town 10 miles north of Durban and employs some 1,400 Indian workers. If flexibility can be maintained and minimal damage inflicted on the chief industrial areas, there should be little difficulty in expanding most of the designated Border regions. Now that the laws forbidding white investment within the Bantu homelands have been relaxed, there may very well have to be a readjustment when trained Bantu workers begin to look for work inside the homeland. The system of Border Regions is also likely to be used by mutual agreement near Lesotho, Swaziland, and particularly near Botswana (when the potential of the northwest Transvaal materializes). Within South-West Africa it has already found favor in certain areas such as Ovamboland, but economic and market considerations will probably predominate here over ideological determinism.

CONCLUSION

These, then, are the techniques associated with separate development as applied to the three non-white groups. Many of them are still bitterly resented within the Republic. In the eyes of some observers, racial discrimination has produced a ludicrous patchwork of irksome subdivisions which are morally indefensible; to others, they seem to be achieving surprisingly satisfactory ends by entirely wrong means. What appears incontrovertible, however, is that the two problems of race friction and of overurbanization, so vexatious still in so many parts of the world, are here being handled in a totally new way, and with some degree of masterliness and success.

It is certainly true that self-respect and national pride are being in some measure restored to the non-whites of South Africa. Some are even beginning to see sense and security in the late Hendrik Verwoerd's vision of a South African Commonwealth of Nations emerging from association of the segmented groups. Economic progress, on a scale barely envisaged some ten years ago, is boosting non-white income and expenditure far above African continental levels. Industrial skills and entrepreneurship have been nurtured in a convenient cocoon which protects the Bantu man from undue competition while he learns his trade or profession. Deficiency diseases such as kwashiorkor are rapidly disappearing. Scourges like tuberculosis have been recognized as unnecessary social and industrial blights.

Few countries outside western Europe, North America, and Australia can boast of being as well housed as South Africa's non-white populations. Education, although still inadequate by the absolute standards of the advanced Western countries, is spreading rapidly among the young; literacy is high and rising; sporting and cultural activities grow apace and occasionally reach the world arena. In their separate areas, each nonwhite group is evolving its own socioeconomic class lines and seeks the usual status symbols of the affluent society.

Each passing day demonstrates to the white South African that his most reliable ally in the difficult years ahead will most likely be these very members of the community whom his laws have segmented so severely.

In this he is helped by the refusal of the International Olympics Committee to accept the first integrated athletic team to represent the country in Mexico City. This may prove a hollow victory for Afro-Asians, who have failed to take into account the well-developed *national* pride of the Bantu; the latter have been deeply offended by this decision, and have taken note of it.

Though race prejudice dies hard, perhaps as hard here as anywhere, there is nevertheless an unmistakable growth of grudging mutual respect between peoples who can at last rely on one another's word and who have been reluctantly forced to admit that their future is one of interdependence. However unbelievable it may seem to the outside observer, there are South Africans, both white and non-white, who have lately observed a perceptible *detente* which, if external agitation can be held in check, may eventually allow the past to bury its dead. More than that, no man can say.

Select Bibliography

H. T. Andrew, *et al., South Africa in the Sixties: A Socio-economic Survey,* 2nd ed., Johannesburg, The Central News Agency, 1965.

Eric V. Axelson (Ed.), *South African Explorers,* London: Oxford University Press, 1954.

———, *Portuguese in South-East Africa 1600–1700,* Johannesburg, Witwatersrand University Press, 1960.

Gwendolyn M. Carter, *The Politics of Inequality,* rev. ed., New York, Praeger, 1959.

Monica M. Cole, *South Africa,* New York, Dutton, 1961.

Allen Drury, *A Very Strange Society: A Journey to the Heart of South Africa,* New York, Trident Press, 1967.

L. P. Green and T. J. D. Fair, *Development in Africa: A Study in Regional Analysis with Special Reference to Southern Africa,* Johannesburg, Witwatersrand University Press, 1962.

Alan F. Hattersley, *The British Settlement of Natal: A Study of Imperial Migration,* London, Cambridge University Press, 1950.

Christopher R. Hill, *Bantustans: The Fragmentation of South Africa,* London, Oxford University Press, 1964.

Hobart D. Houghton, *The South African Economy,* 2nd ed., New York, Oxford University Press, 1967.

Johannes S. Marais, *The Cape Coloured People 1652–1937,* Johannesburg, Witwatersrand Press, 1957.

Donald R. Morris, *The Washing of the Spears: A History of the Rise of the Zulu Nation under Shaka and Its Fall in the Zulu War of 1879,* New York, Simon and Schuster, 1965.

Solomon D. Neumark, *Economic Influences on the South African Frontier 1652–1836,* Stanford, Calif., Stanford University Press, 1957.

Jordan K. Ngubane, *An African Explains Apartheid,* New York, Praeger, 1963.

Deneys Reitz, *Commando: A Boer Journal of the Boer War,* New York, C. Boni, 1930.

E. A. Ritter, *Shaka Zulu: The Rise of the Zulu Empire,* London, Longmans, Green, 1955.

Eric I. Rosenthal, *Stars and Stripes in Africa: Being a History of American Achievements in Africa, etc., etc.,* London, Routledge, 1938, 2nd ed., 1968.

Edward Roux, *Time Longer Than Rope: A History of the Black Man's Struggle for Freedom in South Africa,* London, Gollancz, 1948.

Isaac Schapera (Ed.), *The Bantu-speaking Tribes of South Africa,* London, Routledge, 1937.

C. M. Tatz, *Shadow and Substance in South Africa: A Study in Land and Franchise Policies Affecting Africans 1910–1960,* Pietermaritzburg, University of Natal Press, 1962.

L. M. Thompson, *The Unification of South Africa 1902–1910,* Oxford, Clarendon Press, 1960.

F. R. Tomlinson, *et al., Summary of the Report of the Commission for the Socio-Economic Development of the Bantu Areas Within the Union of South Africa,* Pretoria, The Government Printer, 1955.

Eric A. Walker, *A History of Southern Africa,* London, Longmans, Green, 1957.

John H. Wellington, *Southern Africa: A Geographical Study,* Volume 1: *Physical Geography, Climate, Vegetation and Soils, Hydrography,* London, Cambridge University Press, 1955.

Index